No. 24
THE SUN RA
ISSUE

SA 24 Contents

- From the Editor

- Sites of Formation 1924

- Sites of Formation 1948

- Sites of Formation 1972

- Sites of Formation 1992

- Sites of Formation 2020

- Exquisite Corpse

CONDITIONS AND APPRECIATION   4
Nate Wooley

MARSHALL ALLEN AND THE CREATION OF A NEW WORLD   10
Jessie Cox

GLENN BRANCA'S SYMPHONY NO. 13 "HALLUCINATION CITY"   16
FOR 100 GUITARS AT THE WORLD TRADE CENTER PLAZA JUNE 13, 2001
(EXCERPT FROM A MEMOIR IN PROGRESS)
Reg Bloor

MY TEACHER'S TEACHER—TALES OF CHIEF DEE   22
Taylor Ho Bynum

SUN RA AND DUKE ELLINGTON: PARALLELS IN PRACTICE FOR THE   32
20TH-CENTURY LARGE ENSEMBLE
Ken Vandermark

ACCORDING TO SUN RA, NONE OF US ARE REAL.   42
Naima Lowe

THE EXECUTION OF SUN RA (VOLUME II)   46
A CONVERSATION WITH THOMAS STANLEY
Luke Stewart

ANYTHING CAN HAPPEN DAY: SUN RA, ALTON ABRAHAM, AND THE   60
TAMING OF THE FREAK
John Corbett

FOUR THOUGHTS ABOUT MILES DAVIS'S *ON THE CORNER*   80
Chris Pitsiokos

DEREK BAILEY'S *ON THE EDGE: IMPROVISATION IN MUSIC*   86
Peter Margasak

SOCIAL OR MUTUAL AID MUSIC   92
Nate Wooley

A CONVERSATION   98
Audra Wolowiec with Freya Powell

2020 PART ONE: QUANTUM BLACK IN THE MOMENT   110
Moor Mother

From the Editor

CONDITIONS AND APPRECIATION

Nate Wooley

Appreciation has conditions. In other words, I *like* a thing *because* the conditions of my appreciation, whatever they are, have been met. These conditions act in different ways for different people on different objects. Sometimes the conditions are negligible, because the object of appreciation is just plain likable. For example, only a few conditions must be met for the vast majority of the population to enjoy a piece of pie. Sometimes our love of something has conditions added to it over time, even though our initial experience of it was free and clear. I remember eating the chicken livers my grandmother would prepare. Now, I have to overcome an accrued knowledge of what a liver *is* and what it *does* to be able to eat the same dish.

Finally—and this is the basis of the writing to come—there are objects that we recognize as worthy of appreciation but the individual conditions we've placed on them are almost impossible to meet. My wife hates olives but, for some reason known only to her, she tries to eat one about once a month to see if she can overcome the brininess and unlock the passage to its culinary wonders. Our conditions for appreciation in these instances are, essentially, obstacles that have to be overcome before we can appreciate something; one keeps trying—like my wife eating her monthly olive—because they intuit that the appreciation they are trying to develop is worth the work.

Since I was in my early 20s, I have grappled with my conditions for appreciating Sun Ra. Dozens of people have tried to *help* me—their goal being to bring me into their global community, as in "how do we convince Nate to stop being an idiot and start loving Sun Ra like the rest of us?" The result, while unsuccessful in that I haven't yet overcome my obstacles, has been positive: I'm learning to, at least, define these personal conditions of appreciation.

SUN RA HAS CONDITIONS.
―――――――――――

As I wrote in my introduction to *SA2: The Networking Issue*, I have a hard time understanding the beauty of belonging to any organization. The faintest whiff of a group's hierarchy will have me quietly backing out the door long before I'm able to appreciate what could be gained by its structure and feeling of community. I recognize this is a neurosis built on a lot of historical experiences and my own special brand of irrationality. But, because of that neurosis, some of the most widely accepted signifiers of Sun Ra's greatness—the Arkestra, its communal aspect, his hierarchical place in it—are the greatest obstacles to my appreciation.

Among the other obstacles I have to overcome is my relationship to overt performance. What do I mean by that? I guess I would define it as any action done that is extra-musical and prioritizes dramatic effect over music. While this has become less of a factor over the years, I still harbor a certain distrust of anything that has this *performance* element. This has historically been an obstacle to Sun Ra's music for me. But recently, I saw the Arkestra perform live—my monthly olive—and I could not deny that the costumes and stage performance create a fairly universal feeling of joy. While watching the group parade through the aisles, I understood the sincerity of the spectacle. I turned a corner and now feel like this performance condition is within my grasp—proving to myself that these obstacles *can* be overcome with persistence.

These are the two large hurdles I have to overcome, and there's a lot of work ahead if I'm going to develop my appreciation for Sun Ra. The interesting point to me, however, is that I continue to feel the need to try. If there was something truly distasteful, or even banal, to me about Sun Ra and his music, I wouldn't waste my time articulating conditions and trying to overcome obstacles. So, the question is: what is it, exactly, that keeps me coming back?

SUN RA IS CULTURALLY INESCAPABLE.

For sixty-plus years, the Arkestra—led, since the death of Sun Ra, by the superhuman saxophonist Marshall Allen—has educated and thrilled musicians and audiences. People have been writing about Sun Ra's music, the history and social structure of the Arkestra, and the effect they have had on a strong and vibrant Afrofuturist movement in art and music for decades. There are festivals that celebrate Sun Ra's music, bands that are dedicated to playing his repertoire, re-issues of classic recordings and, of course, the ubiquitous "Space Is The Place" T-shirt found on one in ten jazz festival attendees.

But this saturation doesn't act like viral PR, creating appreciation through saturation and attrition. I don't feel the need to understand Sun Ra's music just because it's there, but because I recognize that it is something special that I should be paying attention to. I may not find that special something in the costumes or cosmic back story. It may not even be in the music for me, but there is something glowing under the surface and I want to know what that is.

SUN RA IS A GENERATIVE INFLUENCE.

The indefinable quality that makes Sun Ra inescapable seems to also be responsible for creating inspiration for expression in others: from a fan announcing their taste by wearing Sun Ra's picture on a T-shirt through the continued creative work of Allen and the Arkestra to keep Ra's influence alive and relevant to all those that take his example as a jumping-off point for saying something new with their own work. Take, for example, Taylor Ho Bynum and Naima Lowe's writing in this issue, both of whom have used Sun Ra's generative influence as a way to push themselves out of their literary comfort zones and onto a new path.

SUN RA MAKES US REEVALUATE WHAT WE ALREADY KNOW.

He wrote a kind of big band music, that after hearing for the first time, irrevocably changes our base knowledge of what big band music is and can be. He even prompts us to take a fresh look at him and his music. In this issue, Ken Vandermark talks about the compositional, economic, and cultural similarities of Sun Ra and Duke Ellington. It's an apt comparison: both are musical figures with compositional voices that were too strong to be contained by the tradition of jazz music. Luke Stewart also talks with Thomas Stanley about his incredible book, *The Execution of Sun Ra*, which asks the overlooked question: "What was Sun Ra trying to tell us?"

SUN RA *CONTINUES* TO BE PRESENT.

Very few artists have an active effect on culture and music long after their passing. Yes, the Arkestra could be viewed as a repertory band, but anyone who has seen them live knows that the feeling is deeper than that. Somehow the spirit of Sun Ra still seems to be in our heads and on the streets. He's found a way to transcend his death by presenting us with an option of being that moves within and beyond the clothing, the intergalactic origin story, and the music. Sun Ra remains a gravity that you either embrace or you fight. John Corbett goes into this in his book *Vinyl Freak*, part of which is reprinted in this issue.

After a rehearsal a couple of months ago, I was riding home with a friend. He was playing memory sticks in his car, one of which was jammed in the stereo giving us two options:

ALL Sun Ra or nothing. My friend knows about my obstacles to, and conditions for, the appreciation of Sun Ra, so he began to half apologize/half convince as we drove down the West Side Highway. And, maybe because I wasn't trying so hard, I started to *hear* Sun Ra's music for the first time. A burning John Gilmore solo here, synths bordering on hard noise there. An indescribably funky off-kilter groove or song lyrics that made me laugh. I was discovering all the conditions that his music had *met* while I was obsessing on which conditions it *hadn't*. I still hadn't overcome all my obstacles or met all my conditions, but now I could *hear* the music, and that gives me energy to keep on trying.

9

Sites of Formation 1924

MARSHALL ALLEN AND THE CREATION OF A NEW WORLD

Jessie Cox

1

1924 was a year that redrew humanity's sense of everything, creating the possibility for new possibilities, a past that can, if taken as a present, rejuvenate. The importance of such a rebirth of possibilities—of the redrawing of the boundaries between impossible and possible—lies in the fact that it allows for other ways of being and for the marginalized to become not only part of the discourse but essential to it. This can only happen if there is another space, another canvas, than the one that deems them as less than real.

One reason why 1924 is important for the creation of new possibilities is that it was the year that Marshall Allen—an indispensable part of Sun Ra's band since 1958 and now, after Sun Ra's passing, the leader of the Arkestra—was born. While showing a video of Marshall Allen's saxophone acrobatics to some of my students—sonic luminescent virtuoso space-travel—the creation of new possible possibilities that first drew myself to his work became apparent (again). Listening to Marshall Allen's musical creations is how I imagine it must have felt when in 1924 Edwin Hubble discovered that there were multiple other galaxies—that ours isn't the only one—in a way giving birth to the universe as we know it today (the second reason 1924 was an important year).

> *Confirmation of the view that spiral nebulae, which appear in the heavens as whirling clouds are in reality distant stellar systems, or 'island universes'... The number of spiral nebulae, the observatory officials have reported to the institution, is very great, amounting to hundreds of thousands, and their apparent sizes range from small objects, almost star-like in character, to the great nebula in Andromeda...*[1]

This description of Hubble's discovery by the *New York Times* makes evident just how world-changing it was. Until that moment, society thought that there was only one galaxy, ours, and that all the other *stuff* was part of that one galaxy. By noticing just how far away these celestial objects are from planet Earth, Hubble recognized that these must be other galaxies, and so the universe's magnitude took on a completely different meaning—and so did our place within it.

Musically speaking and otherwise, Marshall Allen's work can be likened to this astronomical discovery. Suddenly everything is changed, dislocated—one has to redraw the wholeness of the universe because the old coordinate system does not have space for these possibilities that were once impossibilities. What effect does it have on humanity when we suddenly see that there are possibilities outside of our concept of the entirety of space; possibilities that change, by their very existence, our notion of us and all?

A simple and effective way to attune ourselves to how this redrawing of the all is enacted in Allen's work is to focus on the musical instrument as well as his relationality to it. A musical instrument is like a universe. It has its own sound or, more specifically, a sound that the listener expects. An instrument is also a technology, which means that there is a specific way to play it related to how it is built which, in turn, is related again to the idea of how it sounds, since the instrument builder, and instrument performer, have to imagine a sound during their creative processes. For example, the modern fingering systems for woodwinds, with buttons that allow it to cover holes out of reach for a human hand, create a completely different sound, and sound-ideal (as well as technique), than a recorder where every hole on the instrument has to be reachable with a human hand.

These components of the instrument are then further entangled with history, economics, other instruments and tools, philosophy, physics and acoustics, etc. An economic example would be how the timbre of jazz came about. The reason that marching band instruments were so often used in the early days of this music is because they were, at the time of Emancipation, the cheapest instruments around, and most newly emancipated slaves did not have a lot of economic power. Furthermore, during the Harlem Renaissance in the 1920s/30s, more African-American families achieved middle-class status, which allowed for the incorporation of the piano—a symbol of that middle-class status—into jazz, creating the Harlem stride.

Of course, this is a simplified account of the creation of music and musical instruments. It is self-evident that there are a multitude of factors and agents involved with the development of all music and musical instruments. But these examples illuminate that almost all aspects that make up the musical instrument are confined to (or have to resist) the space it is thought to be within, or what society wants it to be. Furthermore, it becomes apparent the degree to which musical instruments and their sounds are *political*. This is nothing new to many jazz musicians since the music of African Americans—from the music of the slaves to early New Orleans jazz, free jazz, all the way to hip-hop—has often been referred to as noise by white American society throughout its history. The consequences of somebody's sound being *heard as noise* and not *listened to as music* are drastic and reach far beyond what is normatively considered music. In the same manner, a musical instrument and its associated so-called proper technique also encodes the dominant culture's values, through its attempts to reinforce itself and justify its dominance. Conclusively, the saxophone (and concomitantly also the saxophonist) is a point of assemblage, of convergence, of an entanglement of history, economy, aesthetics, and more.

3

Through saxophone playing, Marshall Allen defies any previous conception of the saxophone and the saxophonist, and of its entangled components. Via this act he is not only reassessing the musical universe but everything itself. His playing, therefore, has the same effect on society's change in positioning of self, other, and environment as Hubble's discovery that there are many more galaxies in space than ours. The movement of his right hand over the keys reminds one at times of fast, animal-derived kung-fu hand gestures or the delicate brush stroke of a calligrapher, redrawing the size of the keys and of his fingers at the same time. This morphological rescaling helps create, or simply *is*, his stellar-like sound—stratospherically high musical lines with rhythmic punctuations that could be compared to the patterning of the distribution of light-dots on a deep-space-image.

Marshall Allen's body and spirit (his breath) interact with the alto saxophone complex, with what is supposed to have been. Note that we can understand the resultant sonic output from these multifaceted interactions as not only peaceful (or resonating) but at times also violent (or non-conformal). Most importantly this musical respacing changes how society (or at the very least the community around the music) looks at itself, history ("alter-destiny" and/or "my-story" to use Sun Ra's words), economics, culture, etc. The saxophone's fingering-system metamorphoses and its encoded memories and functionalities are changed (hacked). Economic value is taken and redefined because of the "misuse" of the musical instrument; its use value—creating musical sounds—as well as its exchange value is questioned, redefined, and reclaimed. Value and meaning are reassigned according to other laws, laws that are related to the uniqueness of the specific instruments' (acoustic) errors (which, through Allen's repurposing, are not errors anymore). This changes what is valued but also who/what does the valuing and how its value is justified (i.e. its network)—an act of re-networking, re-programming, and re-coding.

The musical approach taken by Marshall Allen could be thought of as utilizing what are called extended techniques amongst today's music experts, but I'd argue that this concept is incongruent with his approach. The extended technique idea relates to a smaller, or different, universe (space), analogous to how our physical universe was seen pre-1924. Allen's playing, as described earlier, moves on another set of dimensional coordinates, meaning that the way these sounds and movements are listened to, and how they are conceptualized/conceptualizable, is fundamentally different than extended techniques, and cannot be seen as something disruptive, unwanted, or as an extension of traditional techniques alone (although it is also a music of resistance).[2] Most importantly, it reshapes the boundaries of the universe by redefining what is to be seen as the extended and fundamental, changing the points of reference/relation. In this sense one cannot speak of extended techniques; these technical reimaginings have to be named, and concomitantly, theorized, in another manner.

"We call it space music. Call it whatever you like, but it's space. It's dealing with, (not these earthly things) those things that we don't know."[3] Marshall Allen's naming and description of his music clarifies the importance of his musical approach. This music that allows for new possible possibilities can displace our earthly worries and make us aware of the vastness and revitalizing force of hearing new possibilities for our existence. It's of utmost importance for a society to be able to re-imagine what *could be* because it changes what *is*, it allows for the creation of other values and meanings, and for the redefinition of oneself. Music, especially Marshall Allen's music, affords this rehearing.

The political implications of this musicking is of great value as well; the repurposing of history and economy via the musical instrument is itself an act of redefinition and possibility-space creation. Marshall Allen's (and Sun Ra and the Arkestra's) music is a space that has places for people and ways of being that wouldn't be allowed, or possible, in the other worlds they found (find) around them. This repurposing proposes a possible solution to the (Marxist) alienation created by not being able to identify with one's environment and creations (not in the sense of anti-alienation but maybe a post-alienation, where post can be conceived of as, on the basis of Afrofuturism/science-fiction, a different future as present and past). Through music-making, Marshall Allen, Sun Ra, and the Arkestra *created* a historical, economical, cultural, and societal space that was different to the situation they faced as African Americans in 20th-century America; and in this same manner this music, and the further pursuit of such ways of musical thinking, can allow us also today to reclaim our own space of existence—reclaiming agency over one's self. As Marshall Allen explains: "You want a better world. You create a better world."[4]

1   Sharov, Alexander and Novikov, Igor. 1993. *Edwin Hubble, The Discoverer of the Big Bang Universe*. Cambridge: Cambridge University Press.
2   For a more detailed account of the complex relationalities that Black musical practices have to the European aesthetic ideals: Gilroy, Paul. 1993. *The Black Atlantic*. London and New York: Verso.
3   Allen, Marshall. 2019. "Out There A Minute With Marshall Allen." PWPvideo. May 23, 2019. Audio, 5:02. https://www.youtube.com/watch?v=GdTR-fiLfwQ
4   Ibid., 6:23.

5

GLENN BRANCA'S SYMPHONY NO. 13 "HALLUCINATION CITY" FOR 100 GUITARS AT THE WORLD TRADE CENTER PLAZA JUNE 13, 2001

(Excerpt from a memoir in progress)

Reg Bloor

Glenn Branca had been asked by the French government to write a piece for 2,000 guitars for their year 2000 celebration in Paris. This concert, of course, never happened because that's completely absurd. The soundcheck alone would've taken a week. But he was paid handsomely to write the piece, which he did not do.

However, the Lower Manhattan Cultural Council (LMCC) in New York had heard about the project and they were interested in staging a large-scale piece of that sort. They initially proposed a more realistic 200 guitars, but Glenn talked them down further, to 100. The piece became Symphony No. 13 "Hallucination City" performed at the World Trade Center Plaza on June 13th, 2001.

I had started working with Glenn the previous year, just a few months after arriving in New York, but this was the first project I worked on with him completely from beginning to end, and it was when I solidified my role as concertmaster and right hand in his operation. This is a role I would serve right up until his death in 2018, and still continue in his absence.

Glenn never started working on a piece before contracts were signed and advances were paid. The contract was signed on May 5, which meant we had five weeks for him to write the piece (which the LMCC didn't know he hadn't yet done), for me to copy the parts, recruit the musicians, and photocopy and send the parts to the musicians in time to work on them (not to mention learning my own part). It would encompass every waking moment.

He wrote the piece on graph paper. Each horizontal square was an eighth note and each vertical square was a half step. He could actually draw the lines of the chord motion. I copied them by hand onto the parts in staff notation because he didn't have time to teach me Encore, the music notation program he used at that time. He'd been using it for so long, he had a two-digit serial number. We never did make a full staff notation score for this version.

This piece was written for nine guitar sections in unison octave tunings:
    four alto sections tuned to two octaves of high E,
    three tenor sections tuned to two octaves of middle B,
    two bass sections in standard tuning,
    with ten or eleven people assigned to each section.

I played the tenor part, the B tuning, as I had for Symphony No. 12, the first live show I did with Glenn in 2000. B is the more difficult tuning because guitar players are so used to E, but it didn't take me long to get used to reading for it. It was similar to reading for the second string on the guitar in standard tuning. The notes on the staff were either played as unison bar chords, or if they had a squiggly line next to them, as half-step clusters. Lee Ranaldo, who cut his teeth in the Glenn Branca Ensemble in the early 1980s (including on Glenn's seminal records *Lesson No. 1* and *The Ascension*, among other early pieces, as well as his first three symphonies), called this chord "the staircase chord," as it was played on successive frets on successive strings in a staircase pattern. The written note was the lowest note in the chord, though you could play it on the top string or on the bottom string of the chord; either way works in this tuning. The clusters in the bass sections were all written either to use one fretted note against an open string or high enough on the neck to play on two strings. But he would stack these clusters into huge walls of dissonance.

The strumming technique was what Glenn called "double-strumming," which was like fast tremolo strumming, but not rhythmic. This was to be done close to the bridge where the string is tight. The effect was a continuous smooth tone, almost like strings. The notes were then let ring and sustained through the rests.

We set about recruiting the musicians by contacting friends, friends of friends, and their mailing lists by email chain. They had to be able to read staff notation, attend two day-long rehearsals in addition to the soundcheck and show day, and bring their own amp. It was a mix of former and then-current members of the Glenn Branca Ensemble (who served as section leaders), downtown luminaries (when downtown was still a thing), strangers who just heard about it, and even some of my old friends who traveled down from Boston, where I lived during the '90s, to participate. We couldn't audition all of those people, so we relied on the prospect of looking like an ass in front of 99 other guitarists to weed out people who couldn't read. We also weren't able to pay them because multiplying anything times 100 becomes a lot very quickly; but we did promise to feed them two meals a day on rehearsal days and on the show day. There must have been about 400 people who contacted us in order to get the 100 we needed to agree to all of the requirements. I wish I'd kept a record of all the excuses. That would be a whole book in itself.

We communicated with musicians by email but had to send the parts by Priority Mail since we didn't know how to make a PDF in those days. I remember feeding quarters into the Xerox machine at the Staples on Broadway in Soho trying to get them all copied before they kicked us out.

This is the first time Glenn had done anything like this with volunteers, so we had no idea if anyone was going to show up. I'll never forget walking around the corner of the North Tower onto the World Trade Center Plaza for the first rehearsal and seeing people sitting there on their amps waiting for us. This was really going to work.

Eighty-five musicians showed up to play the piece. We learned that if 100 people confirm and reconfirm that they will definitely, absolutely, 100% be there, 85 will show up.

The stage was between the towers, with the North Tower behind us and the South Tower on our right. We sat in rows according to section, altos on one side, tenors on the other, basses on a riser with the drums in the back. Glenn was conducting the piece himself, in his manic, interpretive dance style that was more to pull the performance out of us by sheer force of will than to give us any cues. Fortunately, he had long-time Ensemble member John Myers giving a cue every ten measures for when the musicians lost their place. Yeah, that's *when* not *if*. Playing with Glenn is like stumbling after a freight train; no one's listening back to you and no one's waiting for you, you just have to keep up—for 960 measures.

The piece was a swirling cauldron of consonance and dissonance, like a giant swarm of bees trapped in a cyclone, the single movement a long, gradual build of dynamics, pitch, and tempo to a crescendo bouncing off the towers and ringing through the plaza, spilling out onto the streets of Lower Manhattan. It's a sound that stays with you for the rest of the day after the piece is over. You hear it coming out of the subway tunnel or in the air conditioning. You can't get it out of your ear until whole world starts to sound like Glenn.

We got a rousing standing ovation from the crowd. The corralled-in seating area was full, standing room only, though not nearly as many people as the number who claim to have been there. Security tried to keep spectators in the designated area, but they were unable to stop bystanders and passersby from gathering to find out what this sound was.

Afterwards, Glenn held court in the green room inside the North Tower. He answered questions and expounded on his theories of music, literature, politics, and whatever else he felt like, while a gathering of the musicians listened intently. Glenn was a talker. He could go on for hours and people wanted to listen to him for hours. He had a kind of charisma that made people want to follow him, even though he had no interest in amassing followers.

Glenn was initially skeptical of this 100 guitar format. He assumed it would be too muddy sounding to write a piece of too much complexity, so he approached it the same way he would have one of his nine guitar pieces. However once he heard it, he realized the parts were a lot clearer and more transparent than he thought they would be.

After years of trying to break into the orchestral music scene to no avail, he realized he finally had his orchestra.

Glenn completely re-wrote the piece from scratch in 2006 (and continued to tweak it for two years) using tricks and techniques that he had wanted to use with an orchestra.

The original version of the piece was only played once more in a 2004 recording session that was never released because of technical problems, but was notable for including the very young Annie Clark and Tyondai Braxton.

For nearly three years we played the new version of the piece all over the world with what must've been nearly 1,000 musicians. A live recording from the 2008 performance in Rome was released in 2016 on Atavistic Records. That version has nothing in common with what we played in 2001.

If you weren't there, you didn't hear it.

MY TEACHER'S TEACHER—TALES OF CHIEF DEE

Taylor Ho Bynum

At first I did not like him.

It was my second year as an apprentice. The first year of study had been in my own village, with the teacher who raised me; this was my first time away from home, other than traveling to festivals with my whole family. The other students were easily seduced by Rohi's unorthodoxies: his casual dismissal of the most popular songs, his way of melting familiar rhythms and melodies until they became liquid and malleable, his insistence on meditation before and after we played. But I was slow to warm to him. Raised on technique, I was suspicious of anything that hinted of spiritualism. I craved speed and energy, while he talked about sound and silence. The songs I'd spent all summer blistering my fingers to play at furious speeds, he took as ballads, drawing out the spaces I wanted to burn through.

I remember the day my feelings changed. The images are as clear as the sounds to me—perhaps they entwined to knot in my memory—so I know it was late fall. The trees were crisp with color, dark reds and brilliant oranges. We had started studying with Rohi after the summer festival, so I'd been there three or four moons, and I still didn't believe he had anything to teach me. It was a free day, a glorious one, and I had left my friends leaping off the rock cliffs into the lake, shouting out in harmony while in the air, before gasping staccato yelps as they hit the cold water. I already loved most of my cohort, my fellow nascent Wanderers, but I also needed my time alone. I drifted from the group, following a vague path along a brook winding into the forest.

Until that day I never really wondered what teachers did in their free time. I never thought that an elder might enjoy the weather as much as we did, and might want a moment of solitude from my chattering peers as much as I. So Rohi was the last person I expected to see—or first, hear—on my walk. He rarely sang in classes so I didn't recognize his voice. That came to me first, not just carried by the wind but in tune with it, rough and transparent at the same time. It was a Chief Dee chant, but at half the tempo I was used to. Even from a distance, I knew to give it respect; I slowed my pace and lightened my foot, so my approach was muted. As I got closer, the bass snuck in on my awareness, with the rattle of the gourd on the slaps. It was a different vamp, a five-beat pattern (really ten with the double time) we used for movement formations, but that I'd never heard used in song, and especially not against the slow four of the chant. But it wasn't the math that impressed me (I already prided myself on my fractions and polyrhythms). Both strands of music were wholly recognizable, but wholly transformed. Each managed to float out of time yet in time at once. They didn't resolve to the same tonic, they didn't resolve to the same down, but the rub felt correct. Only when I stopped moving, when the path turned into a clearing and I saw Rohi sitting on the ground, did I hear the rest of it—how the breeze set the tempo, the leaves buzzing along with the rattle, how the stream complicated the rhythm as much as the strings, how the melody stretched into the sunlight like a cat pawing the air after a nap.

The music ended—or it didn't, because the wind kept blowing, the trees kept singing, the water kept dancing. Rohi's eyes were closed, and as he opened them, he spoke in a low voice. "Ana. Thank you for listening." (Or did he greet me before he saw me?)

"Teacher, I am so sorry to have disturbed you, I did not mean to interrupt..."

"No formalities, no worries. It is a free day."

I stood without speaking; he continued to sit. My mind worked through confusion—the music had left me vulnerable, changed, curious. I may have managed a stumbling "May I ask..." when Rohi gestured I sit down. I could not yet talk about the spirit, so I started by asking about the details.

"That rhythm against the Chief Dee chant... I never heard them together before."

"Dee actually wrote the rhythm, too—and that's the way he usually played them, together like that. The elders split them after he died. They didn't think the local singers or dancers could manage them at once. Most folks have forgotten."

Chief Dee's time seemed so impossibly long ago, maybe a hundred festivals in the past.

"Did you get to actually hear Chief Dee?"

"I played with him for almost ten years. Near the end of his journey."

I had met ancients who would drone on about Chief Dee at any mention of the name, detailing every time they had heard the original Wanderers, basking in memories of something we could only imagine. Yet Rohi hadn't bothered to say anything about being part of the band for a decade? To his own students? Of course we had talked about the music, and traded tall tales about the legend—but was that mostly amongst ourselves, the apprentices, on our own? My surprise must have been evident. Rohi looked at me, chuckled, and began his story.

"You wonder why I didn't tell you before. I've been teaching a long time, and like any old teacher I have my tricks, but I talk about Dee to very few students. But he taught me to trust my instincts and trust the coincidences of fate. There's a reason you found me today. I like how you challenge me, have your own ideas. But sometimes you make up your mind too quickly; that's a danger of being smart. You forget to listen. So I'm going to ask you to listen now, indulge an old man as he tells you a story...

"There are so many myths, so many fables, people forget Dee was a man once, as I was a boy. By the time I was your age, he was an elder, but he was still strong. He was rather small, almost delicate in build, but seemed much larger just by the force of his presence, his conviction, his leadership. They say he was connected to the old magic. Well, I never saw any special powers—but he was a real scholar, he searched out forgotten knowledge, he listened and remembered more than most, he had deep intuition. He was one of the better musicians I ever met, and maybe the greatest improviser. We all learn that improvisation connects us to the present moment, but he would improvise with the past and with the future. He played the high strings and the harp and whatever else he could find, but his real instrument was the band, manipulating and inspiring and corralling a mess of individuals into one extraordinary, ever-changing sound.

"The traditions weren't set when I was young. The tribes were just forming; my own parents could remember the times before. It's not quite true that Dee's were the first of any Wanderers. There were other bands that came out of the end of the Struggles, and they all crossed paths in those early years. They would sometimes swap musicians and share songs. At first, after so many years of pain and loss, the music was just needed for healing. But soon the Wanderers took on other roles, since musicians are often the bravest travelers. They carried messages from one village to another, they brought seeds and medicines, news of births and deaths, they brought hope and connection. As the tribes became more established, the Wanderers initiated the festivals to bring them together and celebrate the fact of our survival, something that seemed impossible just a few generations before. There wasn't the kind of apprenticeship you have now. In those days, you learned to play in your village with your friends, and if you were good enough, the next band traveling through might sweep you up. They would be your only teachers, and the groups stayed on the road forever. They would have laughed at the idea of eight-year terms.

"When I joined his Wanderers, Dee was old enough to be my grandfather, had been traveling since before my father was born. He was notorious, not revered like he is today; warily respected for the quality of his music but considered a questionable influence because he broke so many taboos. He claimed to be a child of the Earth, born from no womb; he said he brought messages not just from other tribes, but from our ancestors in the past and our descendants in the future. His musicians followed him over any clan or tribal bond; they wore outrageous clothes and sang words that were undecipherable riddles. But among the musicians I grew up with, we heard him and believed. Not the words he used to pull in the crowd. We didn't care about his stories; we didn't care about the costumes and the pageantry. The sound is what sucked us in—it was unlike anything we had yet experienced. It was free but it had rules. It was scary but it was beautiful. The rhythms seemed to emerge from the ground and compel us to dance. He was there for the whole festival, and we were at his feet every night. After the music intoxicated us, the words began making more sense, the sermons between the songs. Of course he came from Mother Earth, of course the symbols on their clothes vibrated with ancient knowledge, of course we had to build an ark of sound to float through the waters of time.

"There was that indolent haze of festival time. Young people in twos and threes and more catching arms, stumbling and laughing to beds or mosses. The optimism for the new days among the younger generations, and the mourning of the past among the older. And feasts, such food—the crops had only recently recovered, cooks delighted in the variety after so many lean years. My friends and I played in the street for scraps and leftovers, in the daytime, when the village cleaned up the night before and prepared for the next. I was playing all the strings, especially the bass. We would see some of his Wanderers in the streets, sometimes even listening to us.

"One afternoon, we were trying one of Dee's melodies—picking it out, a half-remembered groove from the night before—when one of his musicians pulled out his shell and began playing along. Dee's percussionist grabbed a frame drum and boosted the energy, adding his voice and stomping his feet to the rhythms. I swear, we levitated. As much as I've done since, even with Dee, I think that first time with Ori and Levi remains my happiest moment in sound. Though I loved the friends I learned with, I had never played with musicians like that before—without a word, they showed me what we had missed in our self-taught attempts; the intervals and patterns locked into place, the puzzles started to solve. And people could hear it! A crowd began to form, people started to dance, our neighbors tickled to see us young ones playing with real Wanderers. I couldn't tell how long we played, time had loosened its hold. Long enough for sweat to burn my eyes, for my fingers to throb, but I felt no pain, could not stop, the chant would finish when it was done. Finally Ori introduced a slower melody as Levi expanded the beat and calmed the energy; through their sonic guidance our extended eruption settled into silence, only broken by the whoops and compliments of the assembled audience.

"The listeners gave us more food than we'd ever seen—enough to ask Ori and Levi to join us. The Wanderers weren't shy and sat down to eat and regale us with tales from the road. But while my friends were too thrilled by the excitement to notice, I had good enough ears to know how much I had not been able to do... the moments when I couldn't keep up, how much I needed to improve to really play with my heroes. After the meal I pulled Levi aside to ask for help, and he smiled like I had passed some secret test. 'The Chief told us you might be ready. He dreamt of two basses, a moon in the sky and one reflected in the water. Join us tonight. You won't play much, you're mostly there to learn, but when you hear what the music needs sound it with confidence.'

"That's how it began. That might have been the clearest verbal instruction I received in ten years. Levi was Dee's confidante and conductor my first years in the band, translating enigmatic instruction into disciplined action, but even he spoke more of reflected moons, of vibrational energies, of harmonizing the wind, than complex meters or song forms or keys. It was all in the music—the codes and metaphors offered a way to talk about the sound without talking about the sound—technical analysis of Dee's genius would have felt like sacrilege. Or at least so it felt at the time. Now I fear the wild stories are all that's left, the music's been stripped of the layers it carried. It's now simplified and utilitarian and still beautiful, but not as thrilling and dangerous and gorgeous and weird.

"I finished off the last nights of festival on stage, to the eternal envy of my village friends. I didn't play much, but a couple times I heard a space that needed to be filled, or a pocket that needed to be strengthened, so I did my part. Dee barely spoke to me, I didn't know if he even knew my name, but he seemed to accept my presence, and Levi had my back with nods and gestures and unspoken support. The other bassist, Karso, was gruff at first, but my clear respect (bordering on naked adulation) might have won him over. I kept to my place and absorbed how he played, and if Dee dreamt of two basses, who were we to disagree? After the last night, Levi simply asked 'You in?' The next morning I made my farewells to my family and friends, and became a Wanderer. The group just enveloped me, a flock of birds adding one more sparrow to its shifting, flying mass.

"Dee worked us hard, hours of practice when we weren't traveling, but the older musicians reminisced about week-long rehearsals in the distant past, necessary marathons to create the music for the first time (and perhaps find escape from the last spasms of the Struggles). We never saw him sleep a full night, he was the last to bed and the first up in the morning, but he would nod off in naps, even in rehearsals or in the middle of talking, though he claimed that's when he was in conversation with invisible forces. While sometimes he seemed content to let others run the ship, other times he was engaged, demanding, fully inspired. He was also obtuse; he never gave clear directions, instead going off on tangents that seemed barely related to what we had just played. He would say the Struggles were caused by humans misusing the old magic, losing touch with the Earth's needs, and our job was to rebalance the world through sound and vibration, to reclaim, to reinvent, the rituals that were lost. I saw those in the group decades older than me nod along, ask the questions they already knew would never be answered, continue to be attentive disciples with this ephemeral gospel near memorized. Even as I began to recognize some of the lectures, the rants, and could almost sing along, he always mixed in new nuggets of ideas, new plays on words, new cracks of revelation. He knew his chants, but always improvised on them. He was funny! People forget that now, the words have become rote, but those words were first spoken with a hint of a grin and wink of the eye.

"He built his own instruments when he heard new sounds. By the time I joined, the band dragged a cart full of sonic mutants—horns with vibrating spokes hanging off the sides like tired limbs, two-headed gourds that melded lutes with drums, tiny rattles and shakers and massive tubes and gongs. Sometimes he would have us all play instruments we barely understood, raw sounds from untrained lips or clumsy fingers. He wanted us to strive towards mastery, but never forget what it felt like to be a beginner. It was a big band, ranging between twelve and twenty players over my years with them. Partly that was a holdover from the early days, when the roads were still dangerous and there was safety in numbers. But Dee would not have been satisfied by the small size of Wanderer groups today. His sound needed a cacophony of voices, to demonstrate the generative chaos of all at once, and the joyful discipline of all together. And I think the big groups hid his essential loneliness. As charismatic as he was, I'm not sure anyone could really get close to him, especially as his peers died or drifted away, and the Wanderers around him were a generation or more younger. We all wore masks for the performances, exaggerated and grotesque faces embodying the spirits and angels and demons we were trying to summon through the music. But even when he removed his mask, Dee was always in character, always protected; he had masks beneath masks beneath masks, never truly vulnerable except in the music itself.

"The group expanded with singers and dancers at some festivals. Naja, a woman with the Wind Tribe, often sang with us, and those were some of the best performances. She might have been Dee's niece if he ever acknowledged a family, though he never wavered from his mythic birth story. But the core of the band was all men, and sometimes the imbalance was obvious. Dee was a gender separatist; as crazy as that seems now, it wasn't too unusual in the old days. He demanded celibacy and considered procreation a sin. He preached that the human species didn't deserve a future unless it changed its ways, that sexual desire was a distraction, a crutch that prevented resolving the past with the present. If band members fell in love, with each other or with outsiders, Dee would exile them from the group. Though I heard whispers he might have abused his power in the past among his followers, in my time he exhibited no explicit hypocrisies to his teachings. But he still had favorites, and that bred hierarchies and competitiveness, petty jealousies and brooding sulks. Maybe we were uncomfortably close to the cult our detractors accused us of being. It wasn't perfect, and it was always intense. It was a response to a more difficult time, but somehow it worked. It survived because in the end we all followed our leader.

"I still don't know if I was, if I am, a true believer. I believe in the music and always will. That is part of my being—that magic still feeds me. Dee was a real leader, in a time that needed leaders, and made real music, in a time that needed art. He was an innovator and an improviser of the highest order. But for some in the band, he was more; he was their prophet, their god, their Chief. Those were the ones who stuck with him the longest. They were not always rewarded for their devotion. Levi's departure from the band is a story for another time, as Dee was often harshest to those who loved him most. I think he was just a man, a human like all the rest of us—that's what's important. A man who carried scars from the Struggles I could never imagine, who could be suspicious (sometimes with reason), who could be cruel (maybe as a defense), who could be wrong. But a man who made music that was as bright as the cosmos and deep as the ocean, music that conversed with the past and imagined the future. Who told stories that had meaning, transforming a terrible reality into a fantastical dream, because the injustices of reality are what seemed so wrong, so impossible, so limiting to him. Who was brave enough and foolish enough and mad enough to think that sound might save us.

"We're in a better world now, and maybe that's partly thanks to Dee, and maybe there's not room for someone like him anymore. The worst of the battles are over, it's a quieter time, we don't need our fighters to be as scary, as strong, as strange. What was once radical has become accepted practice—and that is good for the most part. We teach you his chants in four years of apprenticeship, we have collective bands of Wanderers bring songs to the tribes in organized patterns, we schedule musicians in terms to keep them from losing their minds on the eternal road. We don't have leaders. We have councils and elders and consensus. We teach the history through the songs and the stories. But in making a man into a myth something is lost along the way: the complexity, the contradiction, some of the power and purpose.

"I learned so much from Dee. How to play, how to listen, how to think, how to be, and how not to be, as well. Those lessons came at a cost. The band was my family, there was camaraderie and love and the joy of shared endeavor, but some of those years were very hard, maybe not as hard as the Struggles but not easy. Discord creates some rare harmonies. The music always made it worth it, until the very end when I knew it was time to leave."

I had never heard Rohi speak at such length before; even in class he used words sparingly. I wanted more of the story, but it seemed clear the last years of Chief Dee brought up more emotions, so I was respectful of his silence. I also now trusted this would not be the last time we would talk. After the music he had played, and the words he had spoken, I was ready to truly be his student. After a long pause, Rohi continued.

"And now I teach. How do I teach this music, in this different world? Perhaps I was lucky to come to Dee when he was an old man, but how do I stay true to what I learned when so much was second hand, and when I want to save you from the harder parts of those lessons? I can filter out some of it, the inheritances of a broken age, but that loses some of the truth. I still don't know, after all these years, I still don't know. Maybe that's Dee's point—ask the questions, always ask the questions, and listen hard for the answers, as many answers as you can get. But don't be afraid to find your own solutions, and accept that some things must remain unknown. You'll understand when you're a teacher—and you'll be a teacher someday, I see it in you. And you'll tell this story your own way to your own students. So don't stop challenging me, Ana. Don't stop asking the questions, but take the time to really listen, even if the music sounds strange. Agreed?"

Agreed.

It was a gorgeous free day, the leaves in full color, the stream in full flow, and we sat and listened to the world.

SUN RA AND DUKE ELLINGTON: PARALLELS IN PRACTICE FOR THE 20TH-CENTURY LARGE ENSEMBLE

Ken Vandermark

SUN RA: CHICAGO BACKGROUND

Sun Ra arrived in Chicago from Birmingham, Alabama, in 1946, and worked with Fletcher Henderson and his big band at the Club DeLisa as a pianist and copyist/arranger from the summer of that year until May of 1947. The impact of Henderson's music and this period of working with the band was clearly profound—more than three decades later he was still performing Henderson's compositions ("Big John's Special" on the album *Sunrise In Different Dimensions* [Hat Hut: 1981]). After his tenure with Henderson, Sun Ra remained in Chicago until the autumn of 1960, performing to mixed success with an evolving ensemble that began as an octet in 1954, and which came to be called the Arkestra. The ensemble traveled to Montreal to perform after the Chicago period, then continued to New York City in the summer of 1961, basing activities there until a permanent move to Philadelphia in the fall of 1968. By 1970 Sun Ra and the Arkestra were touring around the world.

The time spent in Chicago laid the foundation for Sun Ra's creative work as a composer, big band leader, theoretician, poet, songwriter, and director of a record label. All of those activities started in that city, as did an increasing emphasis on the idea "Space Is The Place," indicated by compositional titles and song lyrics that included references to outer space, as well as elaborate costumes and staging that indicated a connection to "other worlds." This complex mythology continued to develop throughout a career that spanned four decades, ultimately becoming a central part of Sun Ra's identity. It is in many of the aspects found throughout this period of creative activity that I find strong parallels to the work of Duke Ellington.

ECONOMIC STRATEGIES FOR CREATIVE CONTROL

By the mid-1950s, the economic heyday of the big band was long gone. Sun Ra had just begun work as a bandleader, while Ellington had already been leading a large ensemble for three decades. Both were faced with an economic challenge that few jazz orchestras participating in the big band era of 1935–1945 were able to meet. And yet, both maintained an orchestra over a period of many decades and until the end of their lives (51 years for Ellington, 39 years for Sun Ra). In order for their groups to survive, it was necessary to come up with financial strategies that could adapt to the economic shifts that confronted them throughout their lives.

When Ellington started working as a bandleader, the practice of long-term, well-paid residencies for musicians was common (for example, the Ellington Orchestra's legendary stint at the Cotton Club in Harlem that ran from 1927 to 1930). By the end of his career, the ensemble's concerts were reduced to mainly one-nighters and festivals, forcing the band to travel almost constantly throughout the United States and around the world. This dramatic change in how concerts were booked was necessary to keep the orchestra alive. Their performances often included a medley of Ellington's old "greatest hits," a policy criticized by those who wanted to hear newer material and who felt that these medleys were a way of pandering to the audience. In reality, it was a brilliant business plan on Ellington's part. In just a handful of minutes he was able to generate a large number of royalty payments from hit tunes composed earlier in his career. (For example, at the Carnegie Hall concert on November 13, 1948, the orchestra played a medley that included "Don't Get Around Much Anymore," "Do Nothin' Til You Hear From Me," "In a Sentimental Mood," "Mood Indigo," "I'm Beginning to See the Light," "Sophisticated Lady," "Caravan," "It Don't Mean a Thing," "Solitude," and "I Let a Song Go Out of My Heart," all in nine minutes and 39 seconds.) These ongoing payments helped sustain the band economically over decades. In addition, the medleys pleased older fans while allowing Ellington to get those pieces "out of the way" so the ensemble could spend more performance time on current, less known material. Based on the number of new pieces Ellington and his composing partner, Billy Strayhorn, wrote each year, making room for the new music was clearly a priority.

    Sun Ra did not have the benefit of income generated through hit tunes like Ellington (between 1927 and 1945, with 1939 being the only exception, Duke Ellington had multiple compositions in the U.S. Top 40 record charts every single year[1]), so he needed to come up with different strategies to maintain economic viability. Key to these was the founding of his own record label in 1956 with the assistance of Alton Abraham, just two years after he started to direct his own band. It was a pioneering move for a musician to control the production of their music from start to finish—from the point of composition to the pressing of LPs. Artistic control was Sun Ra's goal but sales of these albums at concerts also generated additional income for the band and for future recordings. Considering that Sun Ra's discography is estimated at over 100 records, that financial achievement is significant.

    Another idea that helped engender cash flow was to build the Arkestra's fan base through an exciting stage show. As indicated previously, the group almost immediately incorporated elaborate costumes and songs with lyrics about otherworldly subject matter connected to Sun Ra's developing mythology and dancing.

Having seen the band perform throughout the 1980s, I can testify that Arkestra performances were designed to be an entertaining spectacle, visually and sonically. Without question, Sun Ra figured out how to engage people who might never listen to the Arkestra's music on their stereo at home; the pageantry and chanting songs bridged a gap that often exists between entertainment and art, and allowed audiences to navigate between the two as they chose, in a remarkable way.

MID-20TH-CENTURY STRUGGLE

Though different, the economic strategies utilized by both Ellington and Sun Ra were successful from both a business and creative standpoint. The early to mid-1950s was a challenging time for both bandleaders, but they remained determined to find independent means to maintain a large ensemble for their ongoing work as composers, activity that never ceased or slowed down until illness late in their lives took hold. Sun Ra was just getting started in Chicago, and though he recorded several key albums during that mid-1950s period (including *Sun Song* and *Sound of Joy* [both later released on Delmark] and *Jazz in Silhouette* [Saturn: 1959, later on CD through Evidence: 1991]), the history indicates that the response from Chicago's critics and audiences was less than receptive.

The perception of Ellington's work as a composer and the reputation of the orchestra was at perhaps its lowest ebb during this time. Two key members—Johnny Hodges and Sonny Greer—had left the band, and his Top 40 hits had been usurped by the influx of rock & roll. Most of this changed with Ellington's concert at the Newport Jazz Festival in July of 1956: Hodges had returned to the group, and the gig became a legendary part of jazz history. The album created from that concert and studio sessions during the two days following it is the best selling recording of Ellington's career.[2] Aside from a new suite written specifically for the occasion, the material performed at the concert was comprised of Ellington classics, and it was Paul Gonsalves's tenor solo on "Diminuendo In Blue" and "Crescendo In Blue," composed in 1937, that drove the crowd into a frenzy.

With that kind of energized late-career success—so connected to a celebrated past—it would be understandable if a bandleader made the decision to try and replicate that triumph. Ellington did just the opposite, recording the brilliant album, *Such Sweet Thunder* (Columbia: 1957), a month after the Newport appearance. And, in the year 1959 alone, he recorded the soundtrack for *Anatomy of a Murder* (Columbia), *The Queen's Suite* (issued on *The Ellington Suites*, Pablo: 1976), and the album *Blues in Orbit*, which featured a number of new compositions (Mobile Fidelity Sound Lab: 1960, reissued on CD by Columbia: 2004).

EXPERIMENTS IN SOUND AND FORM

Ellington had begun experiments with extended works as early as the 1930s, with "Creole Rhapsody" (1931) and "Reminiscing in Tempo" (1935), that utilized both sides of a 78 rpm record, an unprecedented move for a composer associated with jazz music.[3] This was a full two decades before Sun Ra's rightfully celebrated innovative compositions that included expansive forms, harmony, and texture. Ellington continued to experiment with new sounds and forms until the 1970s. A comparison of two of my favorite pieces from the late 1950s—one by each of these composers—illustrates how advanced Ellington was, a composer whose career began just two years after Fletcher Henderson's, and an artist who never ceased to revolutionize his work.

"Saturn," from Sun Ra's album *Jazz In Silhouette* (1959), is a three-minute and 36-second piece that starts with a mid-tempo piano vamp and an angular, seven-bar horn theme which is played twice. The piece then shifts to a more conventional double-time, big band jazz piece with an AABA form that features great solos by John Gilmore on tenor and either Pat Patrick or Charles Davis on baritone, before returning to the double-time theme, concluding with the opening, angular melody, played once. On *Such Sweet Thunder* (1957), an album celebrating the work of William Shakespeare and co-composed with Billy Strayhorn, Ellington presents a piece entitled "Sonnet to Hank Cinq." It features strategies similar to Sun Ra's composition but covers much more musical territory in less than half the time. The music features Britt Woodman and the rest of the trombone section, but opens with a clarinet figure before shifting to an eight-bar, mid-tempo, register-leaping theme for Woodman. It then moves to a series of two new trombone themes over double time, before bringing back the mid-tempo, eight-bar theme, followed by a trombone cadenza that pushes the instrument into the stratosphere. Though much of the thematic material in "Sonnet to Hank Cinq" is more conventionally melodic than the opening to "Saturn," Ellington and Strayhorn finish the piece with an ensemble gesture that ends on a startling dissonance. To my ears, the organization of the evolving themes makes the structural drama of that final chord sound twice as striking as the opening and conclusion to "Saturn." It seemingly comes from out of nowhere, whereas Sun Ra sets up the angularity of the beginning and ending theme on "Saturn" by laying down a rhythmic and harmonic foundation for it with the piano vamp.

I know of nothing in Sun Ra's catalog from the 1950s, however, that comes close to the invention of another piece on *Such Sweet Thunder* entitled "Madness In Great Ones." During the course of three minutes and 26 seconds, Ellington and Strayhorn move the orchestra through more than a half dozen, non-repeating thematic sections that combine dissonance and an unusual use of rhythm and space, with short connecting interludes, short solo statements throughout, and an echoing trumpet finale that takes place twice, disappearing under Cat Anderson's whispered high notes. The composition is an innovative and completely coherent tour de force of sonic texture—particularly its ending. Though more than six-decades old, if written and performed today it would still sound incredibly advanced. In fact, I haven't heard something as haunting and mysterious in the use of a repeating motif from Sun Ra until the Arkestra's performance in 1970 called "Friendly Galaxy Number 2," from *Nuits de la Fondation Maeght vol. 2* (CD reissue, Universe: 2003). Sun Ra also uses trumpets in a reiterated figure, with static clusters played by flutes over this, while an arco bass solo takes place. Though performed more than a decade later, I find it to be an equally remarkable use of pulse and texture, as beautiful as Ellington and Strayhorn's from "Madness In Great Ones."

The mid-to-late 1950s were not only an interesting and demanding time for Sun Ra and Duke Ellington—they were a period of great transition for the music associated with jazz, a transition that led to a renaissance in the art form both in the United States and in Europe. Many established figures were starting to experiment with form and improvisational methodologies in an attempt to escape the harmonic and structural conventions that had been in place for decades; the trajectory of Jimmy Giuffre's music, for example, from the West Coast School of the 1950s to the pioneering work with his trio in the early 1960s with Paul Bley and Steve Swallow. Other established musicians, like Miles Davis and John Coltrane, were also starting to experiment—in Davis's case with reductions in chord complexity, while Coltrane went in the other direction, creating more density and dissonance in the harmonic permutations. Jazz was searching for something new and more liberating from an artistic and improvisational standpoint, and in some cases it was finally coming around to ideas that Sun Ra and Ellington had already been pioneering in their music.

By the middle of the 1960s the paradigm-shift toward more freedom for the music—maybe best indicated by the impact of Ornette Coleman's groups on the jazz scene—created a ripple effect that transformed the thinking of even mainstream artists. Albums by elder statesmen like Sonny Rollins, Joe Henderson, Freddie Hubbard, and Jackie McLean all explored new ideas during this decade. In addition, this movement created a new avant-garde through the work of the AACM in Chicago in the United States, and developments throughout Europe that were no longer based on American models: in England, the Netherlands, Germany, Poland, France, and Italy. As the 1960s progressed, so did the work of Sun Ra and Duke Ellington.

Ellington continued on his singular path of musical exploration with Billy Strayhorn until Strayhorn's death in 1967, absorbing influences gathered from their travels at home and in countries around the world, which they then integrated into their compositions. (A key example of the creative impact of these journeys abroad, often funded by the U.S. State Department, can be found on the album *The Far East Suite* [re-issued by RCA/Bluebird on CD: 1995]). Perhaps the most radical music Ellington made, however, was without his orchestra or Strayhorn. On September 17, 1962, Ellington went into the studio to record with Charles Mingus and Max Roach, resulting in the album *Money Jungle* (originally released in 1963 by United Artists Jazz, then later on Blue Note). Cecil Taylor stated as early as the mid-'60s, "I never would have thought of playing the piano without thinking it out along Ellington's lines, and that's the base."[4] When I heard *Money Jungle*'s title track for the first time, it was clear just how direct that lineage was. Ellington's use of the piano's percussive capacity—along with a use of dissonant clusters played almost arhythmically against the propulsive drive of Mingus and Roach—is not far afield from the music Cecil Taylor recorded at the end of the 1950s and start of the 1960s with Dennis Charles and Buell Neidlinger. With this album, and the one he recorded with John Coltrane for Impulse! Records in 1962, Ellington showed that he was not only aware of what was taking place at the cutting-edge of jazz at that time—he was part of it.

At the same time Sun Ra was continuing, in one sense, the work began by Duke Ellington in the 1920s by building on Ellington's experiments with tonality, color, and texture in music written for the Arkestra. This was accomplished not only in the ensemble orchestrations, but also by investigating sounds made possible through developments in keyboard technology. Sun Ra added electric piano to his arsenal as early as the late 1950s, and in the early 1960s he was already using the clavioline, a predecessor to the analog synthesizer, while the band utilized more added percussion, "space instruments," and sound makers. By the '70s the Moog synthesizer and other keyboards were incorporated, and the music of the Arkestra included more expansive and abstract material, as well as the songs and pieces rooted in jazz history (as evidenced on the *Nuits de la Fondation Maeght* recordings from 1970 mentioned above). The intersections of all of these territories, often with freely improvised transitions, became a central performance strategy for Sun Ra's music until the end of his career, and is employed by the Arkestra even now, under the direction of Marshall Allen.

REALITIES OF RACISM AND CRITICAL MISUNDERSTANDING

Beyond the indignities and ongoing outrage of racism both musicians faced as African Americans at home and abroad, the innovative music that Duke Ellington and Sun Ra developed frequently came under criticism. As mentioned, Sun Ra left Chicago at the end of 1960 due to the poor reception for his advanced music. And, though Sun Ra and the band took the outer space mythology connected to their work seriously, the spectacle of it could overshadow the merits of the music itself, for fans and critics who had a tendency to look more than listen.[5] Perception of the group's creative activity, however, apparently improved when the Arkestra moved to New York City in the summer of 1961.

Like Sun Ra, Duke Ellington was also met with criticism for expressing his life philosophy through music, and though he called the second of his three Sacred Concerts, "'the most important thing I have ever done,'" "few critics have given them serious consideration."[6] And, though Ellington's invention regarding harmony and instrumental color was celebrated, he was often faulted for work with extended forms.[7]

PARALLELS IN OVERVIEW

It is in all of these ways the creative activity of Sun Ra and Duke Ellington are correlated: their foundation was shaped by musical developments from the 1920s (the case of Sun Ra, by working directly with Fletcher Henderson at the start of his career; for Ellington, through participating in those developments as they took place); they both wrote songs with lyrics in addition to instrumental music, which comprised some of their most popular material; they established their own methods for maintaining the economic survival of their ensembles, which enabled them to continue to record their new compositions and to perform around the world; each was fascinated by the expressive potential of harmony, as well as orchestral color and texture; and both struggled against racism, negative criticism, and the misunderstanding of their work throughout their careers.

Perhaps the most essential parallels, however, are these: they were both keyboard players whose real instrument was their ensemble; they were composer/performers that led big bands for decades during a nearly impossible economic climate for groups of that size; and both created some of the most enduring and important music of the 20th century, which focused on improvisation and continuous innovation, not repertory material from their past. It is in these things—Sun Ra and Duke Ellington's radical invention, problem-solving, and resilience—that makes them a model for creative music in the 21st century.

I'd like to cite John F. Szwed's biography, *Space Is The Place: The Lives and Times of Sun Ra*, New York: Pantheon Books, 1997, as a reference for general details pertaining to Sun Ra's history used in this article.

1   Duke Ellington Discography, Wikipedia: https://en.wikipedia.org/wiki/Duke_Ellington_discography#Hit_records.
2   Schaap, Phil. *At Newport*, liner notes from *Ellington At Newport 1956 (Complete)*, [Columbia Records: 1999]), 19.
3   Tucker, Mark, ed. *The Duke Ellington Reader*, New York/Oxford: Oxford University Press, 1993, 387.
4   Spellman, A.B. *Four Lives in the Bebop Business*, New York: Limelight Editions, third edition, 1990, 60.
5   Tucker, Mark, ed. *The Duke Ellington Reader*, New York/Oxford: Oxford University Press, 1993, 387.
6   Szwed, John F. *Space Is The Place: The Lives and Times of Sun Ra*, New York: Pantheon Books, 1997, 265.
7   Tucker, Mark, ed. *The Duke Ellington Reader*, New York/Oxford: Oxford University Press, 1993, 375.

ACCORDING TO SUN RA, NONE OF US ARE REAL.

Naima Lowe

43

"... Though sympathetic, the judge ruled that Blount (aka Sun Ra) was violating the law and was at risk for being drafted into the U.S. military. Blount responded that if inducted, he would use military weapons and training to kill the first high-ranking military officer possible. The judge sentenced Blount to jail (pending draft board and CPS rulings), and then said, "I've never seen a nigger like you before"; Blount replied, "No, and you never will again."

1. witnessed during the time just before dawn.

dark bodies ... overlap, with the Atlantic always lapping at our shores.
    (of water)
    (of sky)
    (of flesh)

imagine simultaneous teeth grinding, each and every one of us having the same dream, at the same moment, on the same night. that's what it is like to wake up forgetting something that you've never known in the first place. upon waking, our sharpest tools begin to dull as the light of day demands legibility and translation. switch. code. switch switch.

2. scientific knowledge

salinity: dense enough to float a thick thighed body

temperature: warm enough to swim at night in August

depth: everything is in here. yes everything

flora: entire forests and vast decaying cities that can only be seen in dreams.

fauna: when the stars are out, they're reflected in dark water. one particular ocean dwelling species is capable of outlasting all the rest by drinking the starlight as its filtered through the fast moving glassy surface of the water. that substance, fortified and metabolized during sleep, allows the species to see itself clearly for fleeting moments of ecstatic frustration.

3. journeying to space above/space below

black people need scuba gear to breath on land.

4. trajectories: melancholy, hopeful and otherwise.

Sun Ra was sent to prison for refusing to go to war and for being a smart weird piano playing faggot. While there, psychiatrists diagnosed him as being a smart weird piano playing faggot. When he left prison and moved to Chicago, he continued to be a smart weird piano playing faggot. When he began to write the strangest and most beautiful music, he did it as a smart weird piano playing faggot. When he lived in Oakland and then New York, consorting with various black nationalist organizations, he remained a smart weird piano playing faggot. After deciding that he no longer identified with any particular race, but rather sought transcendence to another plane of existence, he just kept on being a smart weird piano playing faggot. Sun Ra became a fixture in Philadelphia in the 80s, where he started to become an old smart weird piano playing faggot. And when he had a stroke in 1990, he kept composing and playing like the smart weird piano playing faggot that he was. When Sun Ra opened for Sonic Youth for a few shows in the early 1990s, he was most certainly a smart weird piano playing faggot. And when he went home to Birmingham, Alabama to see his estranged sister of 40 years, caught pneumonia and died there in 1993, he had absolutely returned to the earth from which he came as a smart weird piano playing faggot.

5. this salty body breaths, fervently.

THE EXECUTION OF SUN RA (VOLUME II) A CONVERSATION WITH THOMAS STANLEY

Luke Stewart

Written in 2014, *The Execution of Sun Ra* (Volume II) is a guide through the effects Sun Ra, as a human being, had on our culture. The works that had previously been written about him mainly focused on biographical information, a specific time period or series of works. In this book, however, author Thomas Stanley calls for the audience, and for the human race in general, to use Ra's life and words seriously. Sun Ra made music for the 21st century while living in and being of the 20th century, and only in recent times has this longtime cult figure entered popular culture. Artists like Solange and concepts like Afrofuturism have placed Sun Ra—his music, his aura, his message—in the contemporary conversation. It is now, more than twenty years after his death (leaving of the planet) that his popularity is at its height with the continued touring of his Arkestra under the leadership of Marshall Allen, and it is the current generation that has embraced Sun Ra's music without ever experiencing the live performance. More than a reflection of his life and work, *The Execution of Sun Ra* is a call to the 21st century—the century of Sun Ra—for abrupt change in mental and physical being for all humanity.

I met Thomas Stanley in 2008 at WPFW 89.3FM, a community public jazz radio station in Washington, DC. We were radio programmers who went back to back in the middle of the night. At that time, our late-night slots were dedicated to people who wanted to showcase more avant-garde forms of the music. Being decades my senior, Thomas reached out to me in many ways as a mentor figure, one who would help me in my early days as a radio programmer. He would share music and we would generally talk about the things we liked. A few years later, we were in a band together called Mind Over Matter, Music Over Mind (MOM^2), using electronic setups for sonic exploration and experimentation. Over the years we have continued to work together on various projects, including some of the research around his book.

Thomas has been a key companion and guide in my own journey through the works of Sun Ra. When he was researching his book, I was also deeply engaged in finding the deep cuts and allowing myself to be influenced and inspired by Ra's words and life. In a way, I was doing my part to help my friend, while continuing to develop my own connection with the music. At the behest of another mutual friend, and through interacting with Marshall Allen and Arkestra saxophonist/bassoonist Danny Ray Thompson, Thomas and I made a trip—or perhaps pilgrimage—to the Sun Ra house in Philadelphia, where we were able to comfortably chat with everyone present and even sit in on a rehearsal.

Thomas has thoroughly researched the works of Sun Ra, including perusing at least two archive locations plus a plethora of other private collections. What was delivered is a narrative of working through how we are supposed to feel about Sun Ra. How can his words and music be applied to our current condition? How do we apply the concepts that Sun Ra spoke about, that his music was about? In an urgent call, the author proclaims early on that "this book must be written now." It is a statement portraying the author's passion for Sun Ra's music but, more importantly, his message.

In the below, Thomas's words are in italics with my comments occurring after in plain text.

ON THE THEMES OF THE BOOK:

Sun Ra as a therapeutic agent to resolve Arrested Development, which was his ultimate diagnosis of modernity. Modernity being everything that starts once Columbus's spawn established their presence in the so-called "New World." Destroy the Old World, take down all the sun symbols that Sun Ra reminded us, and begin the capitalist experiment by stealing Native land and African bodies. So, there was a reason why all that stuff happened, and it happened and now it's time to move on. That's what Sun Ra meant by "it's after the end of the world." So, I looked at Sun Ra as, well, the guy said he was here to help us. What does that mean besides doing great shows and dancing across the stage and outrageous gear? What does that really mean that he was here to help us?
Sun Ra has been compared to Steve Jobs, Jimi Hendrix, and even Jesus. The comparison to the religious character is most important in understanding the author's level of reverence for his subject. It also reinforces the idea that Sun Ra is a catalyst; his purpose was to instill drastic change in society that comes from the study of his concepts and acceptance of the power within. Sun Ra was really here to help us achieve Alter Destiny, a theme to which the author repeatedly returns. It is a concept meaning both "after the end of the world" and that through Sun Ra you can discover the power of changing one's reality.

Sun Ra claimed throughout his life that he was sent here to the planet Earth for a purpose. In really looking at what that purpose is and what he claims within, the author has found a vast amount of material to explore what he really meant by being here to help us. Where most volumes and reflections on Sun Ra focus on his artistic output, his music, and poetry, *The Execution* takes his words at their most literal and examines the implications of that way of thought and being.

ON THE BOOK TITLE:

Volume I is not in print. Volume I of The Execution *includes the works of Sun Ra. He said that the word "execute" has a curious double entendre attached to it. You can execute a man, punish him, kill him. And, you can execute a plan. Put it into action. So, writing, as I was after Sun Ra's earthly demise, I thought it was appropriate to talk about* The Execution, *Volume II as being Sun Ra's plan being moved into action. Volume III is in progress. I'm currently writing a book that is part of the series. Love it or hate it, it will be even one more step removed from simply quoting or paraphrasing Sun Ra.*

Borrowing directly from the vernacular of Sun Ra, the author describes his reasoning behind the peculiar title of the book—a clever title to attract the attention of curious readers and Sunny aficionados alike. Bound by the constraints of capitalism, it is a good idea in a marketing sense. This is also how the author, and perhaps Sun Ra himself, use illusion and deception to attract and stupefy, to entertain.

Upon closer examination, however, the true meaning can be revealed, and it just might be a profound catalytic change. The author is showing how the process of dealing with Sun Ra has changed his being. He has adopted his subject's double-speak wordplay, the mysterious mood, the suggestion of an ever-present deeper meaning. Again, using Jesus as a reference, "Sonny reminded us that the English word *execute* means to put a plan into action as it also means to kill. Jesus, he said, was killed by Pontius Pilate and that *execution* simultaneously put into action whatever plan was attached to the Nazarene's unique presence in the world." Just as Jesus's ideas were executed, the author is attempting to galvanize people around the execution of Sun Ra's ideas.

ON WHAT HAPPENS WHEN WE TAKE SUN RA AT HIS WORD:

I go out on a limb every time I say this. I think that Sun Ra was one of the truly great minds of history. Like a Marx, like a Freud, like all those hegemonic white guys. Einstein, Newton ... The way that those people might have understood certain kinds of social and physical processes, I think Sun Ra understood meaning and value at a very fundamental level. It was very much connected to his word games and how he played around with language, and I think there is in his ideas the possibility of leapfrogging ourselves out of this stasis and over these seemingly impassable problems and actually living the future that we think we're in.

We're not in the future. This is just the 1950s on replay. The only thing that's changed much is the technology. And "yeah yeah" black people can use toilets wherever they want to, and gay people can get married and there's legal pot, but I still would say that socially and at the level of meaning and value, we are moving at a snail's pace. So, I thought that Sun Ra's art and his work was a huge resource for leapfrogging over this stagnation and actually doing something with our lives.

ON AUTHORITY:

I really think, in a painfully embarrassing Sun Ra sort of way, I was chosen for this job. I think that at some point in any number of interactions, he gave me the nod. He said, "I need a lot of people to do stuff for me, and you're going to write that book." The other people can write the other things: the biographies, the examinations of different periods of my life. You're going to write the book that's about the essence of my thought, and you're going to pay for it! (laughs) It's not going to be easy, it's not going to be the popular book, but that's the one you have to write. So, I took that on.

    We listen to Sun Ra—to some of his ideas that he doesn't have degrees in—because he was so amazing at everything else he did. He was so amazing at the tireless effort that went into producing so much music in such a consistent direction for such a long period of time. So, we think to ourselves, well a being that can do all that, maybe they do know something! It's at least worth stopping and listening to an individual who is capable of all that.

    All great black men, whether it's Malcolm or Martin, or your uncle Buddy, or whoever it is (laughs), they pass on and we salute them as "great men of faith." At the church, or the mosque, there they were believing, believing, believing. I think that Sun Ra's energy was an energy of skepticism. Just like every scientist knows that the posture that drives critical inquiry and scientific investigation is disbelief, not belief. Sun Ra understood that we don't play our skeptic card as much as we should because we can't socially. I've found quotes of Sun Ra and put them in the book that never get touched on by the people that say they "know Sun Ra" or "love Sun Ra." He came to nullify all the religions and all the governments. He didn't have any favorites.

    We are born into a social order, and we're socialized into the lies, deception, and fantasies of that social order. That's the truth, whether you're a stockbroker's kid born in the bosom of capitalism, and that's the truth whether you're a beautiful native child living in a hut in an idyllic village in some far-off part of the world. You are born into the lies, the fantasies, the hypocrisies of your parents, and it is taboo to say "damn, that doesn't make any sense."

[It's similar to] Terence McKenna: I'm in trouble already for bringing these two thinkers together. A white guy that promoted psychedelics in a particularly bombastic way, and this Afrocentric icon on the other hand. McKenna said that psychedelics are a way of getting past the questions that we're not allowed to ask. For the questions that are taboo, psychedelics lowers the resistance and allows us to ask them. I suggested that Sun Ra is a forty-year ayahuasca trip for our entire culture, and that his whole purpose was to get everybody to deeply question the authority of the things you've been socialized into, and to see what a world on the other side of that skepticism would look like. Americans like to think that they are the progressive ones, leading the world socially in defeating all the bad "-isms." Every day we come up against evidence that that conceit is unjustified. Every time they close the lid on another coffin of someone killed by police violence or killed in one of these silly, absolutely unnecessary wars, and we're still running around talking about "support our troops." I don't have any troops! I don't have anyone fighting for me, I fight for myself.

We did a fundraiser for ICE OUT OF DC. Somebody has to take a step back and not look at the thing so closely because you won't see the whole picture. So, no one has to remark on the fact that what is happening in the homes of families from Guatemala, from El Salvador, from Mexico, from so many places, it's the kind of disruption that Uncle Tom's Cabin *was written about. That novel created enough guilt and skepticism in American society about the system of slavery that next thing you know, John Brown has started the Civil War. Really when you look at it, here's this big structure that we can't seem to think beyond. People will say "Thomas, Sun Ra was a Republican so he can't be an anarchist." He's a Skeptic. And the nation-state, come on. Where do we get this idea that there is something morally equivalent between someone breaking into your house, and someone sneaking into your country across some imaginary line. Where did we get that?*

I had to do some research on Don Cherry. He was like, these passports, what a bad idea! Where did they come from? We've segregated ourselves according to the colors of flags rather than the color of skin. It's the same thing, isn't it? We want success and improvement within the familiar framework that were socialized in, and those two things are irreconcilable. We want to put out the fire that is burning up the planet, and yet still want to rock our Nikes and drive our SUVs. We can't convert this thing that we're doing over to some kind of non-fossil fuel quick enough, so we have to figure out how to stop and turn and go the opposite way.

The author devotes an entire chapter explaining his personal relationship to Sun Ra, his music, and his philosophy. It has to be stated clearly and honestly, as a relative outsider to the accepted world of Sun Ra research. Having personally met and spent time with Sun Ra himself, as well as members of the Arkestra, goes a long way to winning over the often skeptical aficionado.

In this chapter there are a lot of personal retellings and stories from the author's own history. Entire pages go by without even a mention of Sun Ra. A long story about working in a mental health facility where the author became "well acquainted with the charisma of the insane." In other words, the author is telling the audience that he's seen crazy, and Sun Ra ain't crazy. So that leads us to ask, what if Sun Ra was actually telling the truth about all the things he's saying? Here is where the premise of the book is revealed.

ON DIFFICULTIES IN PRESENTING SUN RA:

One of the things with Sun Ra, compared to any other jazz musician and maybe to any other musical artist period, is that when you add up what the man generated in terms of words from song lyrics to onstage monologues to formal and informal interviews, there's a ton of material to start with. I love Sun Ra, but I don't work from a place of hero worship. I work from a place where he's a guy who's got ideas and what those ideas are. I don't think Sun Ra really wanted to take the time to stop and have a serious debate about his very serious ideas. So, everything was always cloaked and almost self-undermined by the platform of absurdity. Of course, Sun Ra was pulling your leg. How could anybody who looked like that and talked like that be NOT pulling your leg. And I think that was intentional. I think that was Sun Ra's way of saying, look... I'm basically self-educated and I don't think that the world is ready for a Negro to roll up his sleeves intellectually and duke it up with these doctors and scientists and what have you. And yet I think that what he was talking about was the kind of stuff that turned out to be at the top of the list of academic concerns that "serious" people are dealing with. There's this abundance of material and you're wading through it. This guy had an opinion on just about anything you can have an opinion on, and there's so much forest there that you could easily get lost in the trees. So, for me it was kind of like, dive in. And as you're swimming around, reach out and the things that you can internalize, those are the things that will help you float. It was tough. It was hard work because Sun Ra's primary nemesis was death. He saw himself as our champion against death, and this is on a number of levels. On the carnal level, you had an individual who was committed to mastering a craft where if your body holds out you can conceivably just get better forever. And he had to wrestle with it. I saw it in him as a human being. I saw him so disappointed when his body started falling apart. He was embarrassed that his mortality was on public display, and that despite all his efforts he wasn't able to put death in the bag.

The other way to look at it is that, historically, death is the motivational factor to distort how we live. The whole Judeo-Christian premise is that we have a little time on earth and then we die. Then if we've done everything we're supposed to, we have like cake in heaven forever and ever and ever. Our lives are constrained and distorted by tremendous pressures to defeat death by leaving permanent monuments here. Whether those are monuments of a very strict and literal sense like the Washington monument, or monuments like our children, our family, our clan, our social order. These are things that are supposed to outlive us because we are painfully aware of how fragile and short our time is. It just fucks us up and we don't know what to do with it.

The author tells a long story about working at a mental hospital. He was intimately experienced with the mannerisms and behaviors of truly "crazy" people. Based on the author's experience with the mentally ill, he could make an amateur diagnosis that Sun Ra probably was just as crazy as all the other jazzmen of the day. After all, mentally ill genius is the tradition of the great jazz pianists. "So I played with the idea that Sun Ra was a functional schizophrenic.... Thelonious Monk and Bud Powell were both famously compromised."

"Of course, no sooner had I formed my amateur diagnosis, than it had ruled itself out." Ruled out by the fact that Sun Ra maintained an exceptionally rigorous schedule as a musician, bandleader, and businessperson. He is, in fact, a singular figure in the history of music for having held together a band of sometimes more than two dozen people for multiple decades. This level of achievement could not be attained from the mind of a functional schizophrenic. It is here that the author states the case for the authority of Sun Ra himself. Many in the Sun Ra community, even, possess strong doubts about his philosophical activities, preferring to focus instead on the music, which for many is profound and interesting enough. Thomas borrows his authority as a mental health worker to rule for himself and the audience that Sun Ra is in fact not crazy. Therefore, what does it mean if Sun Ra was telling the truth, or at least his truth? Again, the premise is developed here.

ON DEATH:

I think one of the quotes that always stands out for me is that Sun Ra would say to the band, "Other men will ask you to give up their life for them. I'm asking you to give up your death for me."

I spent a lot of time in the book talking about how modern medicine has pushed back the veil of death through all of these new understandings about oxygen deprivation and the brain, keeping people cold when they've had cardiac arrest, etc. You have to wonder, what society would be like if death didn't pose such a hard stop at the end of our time here, and I think Sun Ra is asking a lot of those questions.

ON DEVIATIONS IN TOPICAL ISSUES, EXEMPLIFYING THE EFFECTS OF SUN RA:

I wanted to show how your thought changes when it's been dislodged by a sufficiently strong dose of Sun Ra. I wanted to show how that if you have enough of his thought in your system, all your other thoughts would change. I wanted to show that you don't write about Freud's ideas about the self-conscious and the ego and say "Freud" on every page. You don't write about Marx and his ideas about history and capital and power and say "Marx" on every page. To take Sun Ra's ideas and apply them to personal life and social life proves that they're good ideas. I knew I was running the risk of people saying, "well you know it's not really Sun Ra, it's really you." Well YEAH. That's how applied knowledge works. This is Sun Ra's ideas in my hands, and I'm doing as much as I can with it, and I wrote one book. What can you do? You get some Sun Ra ideas. Take a big dose, get it in your system, let it move around, and then you do something with it. I bet it won't be what you're doing.

If you just take a superficial path, a light dose of Sun Ra, he is extremely suited to a very closed narrow reading of

Afrocentricity. He wore ankhs, he dressed in garb, he quoted Ancient Egypt, "oh my gosh." Spoke in that beautiful Southern drawl. As much as I miss his music, I miss hearing him talk. I miss hearing all that Southern antiquity in his voice and everything that means. I miss it.

When you look deeper into Sun Ra, he wasn't that guy. He wasn't the guy to throw red, black, and green around and say look here, he's just like Marcus Garvey. He really isn't. The notion that Sun Ra's utility, being his value and purpose, was just sort of to give black people another hero so they can feel better about themselves, fuck that. The man had an idea about planet Earth being a place that was in need of development, rehab. It's stuck.

Marvin X Jacmon, a cat from the Nation of Islam, was one of my best sources for the book. He said that what I learned from Sun Ra, and you can see this if you research, everything after Egypt is a reiteration, a watered-down version, of the dynastic order of the pharaohs. Big buildings, big institutions, big ideas about metaphysics, god, eternity. Sun Ra was saying that was great for 3,000 years, and now we've got sequels and they're running out of gas. Now here we are, really into the 21st century, let's do something different. Black people have a roll because of what we've witnessed and still hold memory of in our collective consciousness. We've been androids. You take a human being and make them an android not by ripping out their brain and replacing it with a CPU, you take a human being and you mess around with their programming. The code is just language. And you socialize that human being into thinking that they really aren't a human, and that they can be used here at the disposal of the guy that wrote the program. We've been flesh bots. We've been robots. So now it's like "been there, done that." What's the real future look like?

Power is the antithesis of control.

We need power, but control is not on the table anymore, that's not the objective anymore. Look at how vast the universe is. Our destiny is to interact with all of that. Somebody thinks that the program is to destroy this planet. The elite will build starships and as the planet is dying, they will pack up and get on these spaceships and go out and colonize these other planets. I don't think that's how it works. I don't think we get our permission slip for interstellar travel until we restore this planet.

Sun Ra lived in Chicago, New York, and Philadelphia. People don't think of a man who's identified with an urban lifestyle in urban settings as a naturalist. But Sun Ra was deeply attuned to the natural world and the necessity of our responsibility to be a part of this cohesive whole that includes all the life that's here. I think the next hundred years could be the best hundred years of human history, but we have to put down what's in our hands to pick up the next round of work.

That's the execution, the implementation of Sun Ra's optimistic and utopian vision of what the planet could be.

ON EQUATIONS:

"Had the evidence of Sonny's equational analysis of the planetary condition been limited to onstage and backstage rants, lyrical content, or even his voluminous recorded interviews, we might still be justified in viewing his work as thinker and teacher as simply an appendage to his life as a performing musician, an elaborate epiphenomenon."

Sun Ra felt the need to document his work, more so than any other jazz musician. He sought a full equation between the Music and the Message, his planetary call for evolution.

ON AFROFUTURISM:

You told me that the term comes from a white literary critic. I agree with you that there is something tired and grating about our culture being subsumed under somebody else's label, again. And yet, if you play a bass or a saxophone and you swing, if you don't call what you do jazz, you won't get work. In a positive sense, what I've seen is that Afrofuturism tends to draw together younger black people that I might have more of an affinity with than older black people. I'm a generational outcast. I'm the sixty-year-old black dude that doesn't want to hear anymore P-Funk... and I want to hang out with people who want to solve problems, not just bitch about them. So, in my head, Afrofuturism is Afrocentricity with an upgrade. It's an understanding that socially on this planet you cannot escape the centrality of White Supremacy as the major axis of oppression. But I don't think you can reduce all the suffering and all the contradiction, and all the problems here to an idea about white people punishing everybody else. The historical evidence is that white people cannibalize each other. You can ask the coal miner, you can ask the Northern Irish, there's lots of people you can talk to about that!

> I think Sun Ra's "Afro future" was Alter Destiny. This is where it gets trippy. I think Alter Destiny is a "when" that constitutes a "where." Sun Ra says Space is the Place, but where's the place? The place becomes apparent as soon as we get to the time, and the time is up to us. History is full. Its project was unifying the planetary system through a techno-economic gesture of brutal and sweeping effect, and it's done. The stuff that's leaking out of history is Alter Destiny, and there's going to be more. I quoted Sun Ra in the book saying, "first there's going to be chaos, and then utter chaos, then right then you'll look for the Alter Destiny to step in." I can stand with the "resistance" and be every bit as upset as everyone else about the bigot in the White House. But I can take a step on the Alter Destiny side and say that this is systematic of an empire in decline. This is a dying order clutching at straws, and perhaps when this one is exhausted there won't be anymore.
>
> I ask people to imagine a world without calendars. Imagine getting things done without that grid to place your activity across. Imagine a social order where the expectation is NOT that you'll spend the best part of everyday, except Saturday and Sunday, involved in some kind of economic activity to build wealth. Imagine everything else that we can do above what we've already done. And all of those things are in reach once we click those gears and get into the time that's right here, but we're not aware. Alter Destiny is in the world, but we can't see it yet.

It is useful to remember that the man known as Sun Ra was born Sonny Blount in Birmingham, Alabama, during the peak of racial oppression. Lynchings were commonplace; segregation was the law of the land and the basis of social behavior. White supremacy was frequently on display. Even so, he was a different individual, a weirdo for anywhere, but especially Birmingham in the early 1900s. What he saw and experienced would be conflated into his biographical mythology, having experienced a relative wealth of culture in the Magic City, as it was known.

A man of his time, once he reached Chicago, he was immersed in the burgeoning culture of soap-box, on-the-corner preaching. At this moment, however, it was noted as being a hotbed for grassroots black political, religious, and spiritual revolution. Ra quickly joined the fray, learning as much as he could while also developing and delivering his own brand of revolutionary soap-box talk. His would be about liberation not on the Black Star Line, but on a spaceship.

"... Sun Ra would have to be seen as a black nationalist ... Sun Ra can be neither credibly severed from the African-American tradition nor accurately contained within it ..."

Throughout his career, Ra was reaching out specifically to the black community. From his assisting Amiri Baraka in his early presentations of the Black Arts Movement in Harlem to his participation in FESTAC, the legendary festival in Nigeria, Ra has always been concerned with reaching black audiences with his music and message. He was a true elder statesman for the revolutionary generation of the '60s and '70s, giving lectures and debates to anyone who would listen.

ON ALTER DESTINY:

Sun Ra told me that Alter Destiny is like the vice president. If the president messes up, you don't like what he's doing, you pull him out of there and you put the vice president in. Our destiny is dystopic sci-fi. A planet of very few winners and many, many losers, and technology maintaining that inequality in perpetuity. If you want to buy into that and roll the dice, or position yourself with the elite, you can try it—but there's nothing logical about that. Sun Ra said that you can flip the script and do something entirely different. You can move into an ecology of awareness that actualizes justice, and obviates race, war, money, and the nation-state. Alter Destiny isn't a project that we are executing. The planet really is a spaceship, and Alter Destiny is its preprogrammed and inevitable destination. Resistance is futile.

ON SUN RA AND GOD:

This is a touchy one because ultimately, I want people to like Sun Ra. And I don't think that most people's ideas about religion and God are consistent with Sun Ra's. So, if you really start exposing what he felt about that whole matter, I think you alienate people.

Sun Ra had an acute awareness of how "make believe" for the human being does not simply constitute falsehood, but it can, under special conditions, constitute myth, and myth can be much more consequential than mere reality.

I think Sun Ra was performing for us the dance of Moses, the dance of Isaiah, the dance of anyone who came down from the mountain and said, "You know what God told me? Well check it out." He was performing that for us and doing it in such a campy, kitsch sort of over-the-top absurd way, that we were supposed to get that that's the way it went down thousands of years ago! We were supposed to get the fact that all of those dudes were well intentioned peo-

ple who knew that a little "white lie" could go a long way toward helping people if it was the right falsehood. That's what it's about.

Sun Ra spoke of God the way you might talk about a neighbor that has loud parties or something. He was not one to grovel on the ground and assume a position of passive obedience before the divine. He very much felt like whatever the divine intention is, if we can still speak on that, that's built into the cosmos, that's what you serve. You serve it by being active, by being a creator. Creation is a challenge. Because if you make something and it wasn't there, you're challenging the establishment. If I make a song, and that song wasn't here yesterday, I'm saying that "perfect world" that God created yesterday, wasn't perfect. It was imperfect in precisely this way. It needed my song, and here it is.

It's all about hyper-creativity. Right now, we've created so many different ways that you can use your telephone to order a sandwich. And that supposedly proves how advanced we are. Bring that hyperactivity closer to home. Bring the idea that everything can be improved closer to you. To be creative isn't to follow a trend. Sun Ra is an iconoclast because he didn't stand with anybody. He was not allowed to participate in the closing parade at FESTAC in Nigeria, because Sun Ra wasn't down with everybody having to do the Black Power salute. That's the kind of guy Sun Ra was. Anybody who is into something that is clique-ish and group-oriented should be very careful about embracing Sun Ra as their hero, because that's not where he was at. He was a loner going back to Birmingham.

Birmingham, man. The most segregated city in America. Then there's this young black teenager standing out on the corner in a toga and sandals, giving his own interpretation of the Bible! He took enormous risks. His resistance to World War II. The induction office kept sending him mail, but he thought they had to be joking. Everybody knew he was a musician. He wasn't going to war! He didn't care how evil you told him the other side was, he got business to do. And he paid for it, they locked him up! He wasn't about groupthink. I'm not saying he wasn't about togetherness, because a band is ultimately a band that sounds good to the extent that you can create togetherness.

ANYTHING CAN HAPPEN DAY: SUN RA, ALTON ABRAHAM, AND THE TAMING OF THE FREAK

John Corbett

By the time I stumbled to the phone, the machine had already picked up. "Rise and shine, sweetheart;" crowed a chirpy electronic voice. "Day's getting old!" I interrupted the message, the receiver's hovering proximity to the transmitter instigating a brief convulsion of feedback, before switching the answering machine to "off" and murmuring hello to Vic. "It's now or never," he said. Still dazed, dopey from painkillers, I forced out a question: "OK, wow, that's kind of a big surprise, so what's the plan?" Vic seemed to have been awake for hours and mainlining caffeine. He spoke with flickering intensity: "Today is anything can happen day. Be ready to go in twenty minutes. I'll pick you up at your place." I registered assent. Vic punctuated the call's end with: "We ride!"

It was just after sunrise on a warmish September morning. I was decked out in Chinese silk pajama bottoms. Pulling them out by the elastic band in front, I examined the gauze pad, which had seeped a little with blood and pus in the night. Slipping into a T-shirt and tennis shoes, I splashed cold water on my face, kissed my sleeping wife, grabbed the vial of drugs, and set out for points south, the far South Side of the city that hugs the contour of the lake, into a neighborhood I'd never seen, the home of a man I'd known a little, about a stash of historically invaluable stuff he and I had once discussed. He'd been dead for more than a year.

Three months earlier, on a griddle-hot July afternoon, I'd been sitting in my un-air-conditioned home office, tooling around on e-mail, which then took what now seems an unacceptably long time to load. Among the new messages that oozed its way onscreen was one interestingly headed: "Emergency!!! Sun Ra's Home in Peril!!!!" It had been forwarded twice, once from Mike Watt, bassist of fIREHOSE and the Minutemen, and then from an acquaintance of mine who knew about my abiding interest in Ra. The e-mail's source had been shed in the process of forwarding, but its contents gave a few details: Sun Ra's home in Chicago was being vacated and all his possessions were being thrown into the trash; could anybody help?; if so please write back to Mike. Somewhere in the message, the sender mentioned a film festival and her own name, which was Heather.

It wasn't Ra's house. I knew that because he'd left his Chicago apartment in 1961. But the hidden meaning of Heather's message was clear to me. Alton Abraham, Ra's first major supporter and his manager in the '50s and '60s, continuing piecemeal for decades after, had died nine months earlier. It was Alton's place. I remembered having thought to myself at the time I heard of his death about the mountain of materials he'd told me about—instruments, writings, tapes, documents. I had suggested finding a place to safeguard and archive these precious objects, and he agreed, charging me with finding the right institution. I'd made inquiries, tried to interest the few folks I knew who worked in those sorts of places, but got nowhere. Funny to think from this vantage, but a houseful of Sun Ra ephemera was not, in 2000, considered culturally significant enough to merit the cost of being stored.

Alton's death gave me first pause to think about the fate of these things. After consideration, I decided that there were plenty of people to attend to them, someone certainly would, if nobody else then Abraham's loyal sidekick, James Bryant. So I let it drop. These months later, sweating onto my keyboard, once again I had the same thought: surely there's somebody working on this already, at least from the thousand people who must have gotten the Watt S.O.S. My fingers assumed position to delete the e-mail. But just before I let them follow through, I was seized with doubt. What if nobody's on it? What then? Where will all that shit land? I reopened the message, jotted down the name Heather, and dialed the office of the Chicago International Film Festival.

A few moments later, I was speaking with Heather. She'd only sent the e-mail to her friend Mike half an hour earlier, and I was the first one to contact her, so she was flustered and a little wary. I briefly introduced myself, told her that I'd written about Ra, had spent some time with him on several occasions

She asked if I was free that night, said that she was busy with work. I said yes.

"Meet us at the California Clipper," she said.

"Us?" I said.

"Yeah, there's three of us. Can you be there around eight?" We agreed and hung up. I thought for a minute about the insane speed of today's information superhighway, some idea like that, long since made quaint by the hyperbolic curve that technology's speed has followed in these intervening years. Amused, not thinking too much of it, I went about my day.

The California Clipper was dark and empty. A brown barback with ornamental detail occupied one side of the space, and a small stage with red velvet curtains sat unused in a corner. I arrived first. After a short wait at the front of the tavern, the door swung open and three young women stepped in. One introduced herself as Heather. The others gave their names, and we wound around to a rear booth, the three of them setting up on one side, me on the other, like a tribunal. I had not noticed the banker's box carried by one of the women, but after a slightly more involved round of introductions, Heather pulled something from inside the cardboard container at her feet and said: "What can you tell us about *this*?"

It was a shallow wooden block with a swath of metal affixed to one side. A print plate. I felt its weight in my hands, spelled out the words backward, controlled my excitement, and said: "This is what they used to print the record cover for *Other Planes of There*, which came out in the mid-1960s." I put it down. "I know you think this comes from Sun Ra's house, but it doesn't. If you look, you'll find some of what you have has the name Alton Abraham on it. The three women looked incredulously at one another; one reached into the box and put an envelope on the table.

Heather said: "How'd you know?" I examined the envelope, which was addressed to Abraham, the return address: Sun Ra in New York City.

"I knew Alton. He passed away a while back. They must have sold his house." They pulled more items from the box, and I identified them and gave a little lecture on each one, puffed up with the thrill of the moment. A note from Ra to Alton discussing possible record covers. The original drawing for the cover of *Discipline 27-II*. Assorted sketches with Ra and the Arkestra spelled out on them. A couple of record covers with space themes. I remembered the last meeting I'd had with Abraham, at Valois, the diner in Hyde Park with the greatest motto: "See Your Food." We had chummed around talking nonsense as if we'd been buddies—his voice so deep and cavernous it seemed to come from somewhere inside his large frame rather than his throat. I sensed a longing for camaraderie that might not be so alien to the predisposed loner.

"This is so incredible. You don't know how outrageously important this stuff is," I said, returning to the print block. "It took me five years of hunting just to find a finished copy of this record with an offset cover, and then I had to pay two hundred dollars for it, it's that rare. And here we are looking at the printmaking device that they used to hand-make the initial pressing in Alton's makeshift basement facility." I straightened up. "The history of DIY music production, the lost early logbook of the most important jazz big-band leader since the 1960s, one of the great visionary artists of all time. This is the root of it all!" The box emptied, we sat looking at its contents as a delayed round of drinks finally arrived.

"A friend of mine is a picker," said Heather. "He knows everything going on demolition-wise on the South and West Sides, and when something's being torn down or emptied out, they know where to find him. He got a call to salvage this place, but there wasn't anything valuable in his eyes, no modernist furniture or cool old fixtures, so he declined. Knowing that I liked spacey stuff and weird kitschy images from the '50s, he bought a handful of things from them and gave me my pick of the litter. I saw it and flipped out because I knew it was Sun Ra and I knew we had to save it."

Heather sipped her drink, and one of the other women spoke. "We sent out the e-mail, and here you are, as if we had called you. Or sent up smoke signals."

"What do you intend to do with it?" I asked.

"None of us has the expertise or inclination to do much of anything with it. That's why we went looking for the right person. Seems like you're the right person."

"I would be honored. The main thing would be to keep the bulk of it together. Break it up, and each part doesn't mean as much. I'll pledge to do right by it, whatever that ends up meaning." I leaned back, contemplating the most outrageous single acquisition that I would ever make with an unwarranted sense of circumspection. I still had no idea where this would go. I was pleased that I had not hit delete.

Heather selected a single object from the pile and said: "I want to keep one thing. Nothing too important, but a souvenir to remember this."

Sensing the end of the inquisition, the third woman moved to my side of the booth and proposed a toast: "To Sun Ra, wherever he now resides."

A few days later, I was in Vic Biancalana's backyard. Mats Gustafsson, the Swedish saxophonist, friend, and fellow record fiend, was in town for a gig, and he accompanied me on the visit. After hellos, during which we learned a little more about our host's work, including his greatest prize, which was vintage stained glass and historical terra-cotta, we retired to Vic's garage, where he storehoused and assessed his scavengings.

I liked Vic at once. Shortish and solid in stature, he was coarse, tough, and charming and spoke with an unrelenting Chicago accent: a working-class Italian American guy who panned the grounds of the city's once-opulent-now-destitute neighborhoods as their edifices were crumbling. He had a gentle smile cocked to one side, the genial hustler, and he spoke of things he would sell and ones he might keep for himself based on his wife's predilections. "She's the boss," he said, tongue only partly in cheek. From the lilting way he talked about his job, I got a feeling from him that Vic and I were of the same school of thought about material culture. We were both zealots of stuff.

Momentarily distracted by a pile of seven-inch records—Vic offhandedly told us we could have any of them we wanted—we surrounded a big olive-colored chest. "This is what I got," he said, pulling open the top and revealing a small container full of Ra paraphernalia on a par with but more bountiful than the Clipper unveiling. Mats and I rifled through the things, holding back gasps and shrieks as we uncovered more print blocks, El Saturn Records press releases from the '50s, and a business card for the Cosmic Rays, one of the vocal groups that Ra coached.

"Heather mentioned that you turned down a full-on salvage," I said. "What are the chances of you reconnecting? You think the house has already been emptied?"

"I drove by the other day, and it's as was," said Vic. "I don't know if she got someone else working on it, but I can try to find out. Might not be easy, though. One thing them asking you, another you asking them."

"How much for everything in this box?" I asked. We settled on a price; I cut him a check and loaded it into my car. Vic said he'd work on being in touch with the woman who was selling the house.

"It's been sitting there empty for a year, so we may have a little time. But if it's already sold, maybe they need to be out. We'll know soon enough."

Six months earlier, on the racquetball court with my cousin Tim, I had noticed a bulge in my shorts. Ignoring it for as long as possible, I had the hernia diagnosed and fretted about it endlessly, as only a good Eastern European boy can, ultimately by pretending it didn't exist. By the time of my initial meeting with Vic, the little inguinal bugger had become a pest. Weeks passed. I imagined that Vic would call and soon we'd be on a big haul, which gave me a great excuse to put it off. Every few days, I'd check in, and he would tell me he was working on it. I drove to his house a few times to look at other scores, some cool Prairie School chairs, a set of terra-cotta lions he'd extracted from the top of a building. The latter he was forced to give up by an alderman who threatened to shut him down if he didn't put them on her front lawn overnight. The island of misfit toys or the mafia of reclamation—sometimes it was hard to tell them apart.

Wondering about the potential contents of the house, I called an East Coast record producer I knew who had dealt with Alton. He said he hadn't heard anything about Alton's place being cleared out. "Anyway, it's nothing, I'm sure," he said.

"Nothing? You don't even want to check to make sure that important historical material isn't being trashed?"

"Let me make a few calls," he said. A week later, I called again. "I checked and it's nothing, it's shit. Nothing but forty years of junk, no tapes, nothing significant. Shit shit shit. Nothing but shit, you hear?"

I let his weird rant die out. "Yep, I hear you loud and clear." I knew four things for certain: (1) it definitely wasn't shit, there was something important at Alton's, maybe lost tapes; (2) it was of great historical significance; (3) he was after it; (4) I could never trust that guy again.

However, after six weeks of effective procrastination, I admitted to myself that the likelihood of salvaging the house was dimming and that I should schedule my surgery. Vic said he'd been in touch and they were "considering his offer," the specifics of which he would not divulge. But still time dragged on, and I steadied myself to go under the knife.

My father-in-law was the one person I knew who was experienced in the hernia surgery department, and his advice was not to worry, that he'd been up and at 'em later the same day. This seemed far-fetched to me, but it gave me courage as I was prepped and shaved and drugged. "Let's give him a really fun trip," I remember one anesthesiologist saying to another as the spike hit my arm. "Count backward from one hundred." I didn't make it to ninety-seven.

Experiences vary wildly, I learned, and I could barely stand up by the second morning. The second night my penis turned purple and I made a panicky call to the nurse, who said it was normal, happens all the time. "If there's even a remote chance of this happening," I grumbled unhappily into the receiver, "then you must tell the patient about it! It's terrifying. I thought it was going to fall off."

On the third morning, slightly better, upright at least, I stood on my front porch waiting for Vic. His pickup rolled alongside the curb, and I hobbled over and climbed in.

"Morning!" he said, handing me the joint he'd been toking. I shook my head, jiggling the plastic pill bottle at him.

"I'm high enough already," I said.

"Yeah, nice getup," he said, regarding my PJs quizzically. "What happened to you?"

"Hole in my GI. They had to patch it up."

"Should you be lifting?"

"Definitely not. You think you can handle it, let me play supervisor?"

"With my crew, no problem. You're the boss."

"I thought your wife was the boss."

"You see her here?" He flashed me a wolfy grin.

We made our way to the Kennedy Expressway, which was still clear just as the sun was snapping to attention. At the city, we off-ramped onto the Dan Ryan—Dangerous Dan, I always heard it called—populated by barely held together 1970s American cars with no suspension going the speed of lowflying jets and changing lanes at random intervals. I glanced at Vic's hands on the steering wheel. Harsh and sandpapery, clenched vices, they were the hands I'd learned to associate with heavy duty junkers. Nothing to mess with. Unconsciously, I rubbed mine together and thought of their baby softness, which signaled privilege and life choice; the tips of my left fingers were calloused and stiff from guitar, a bit of my hands empathizing with Vic's.

At Forty-Seventh Street, we exited the highway and headed east. Looping around, Vic stopped for a few minutes at Valois, the very same diner, and grabbed us breakfast and coffee to go. Back up on Forty-Seventh we pulled up to King Drive, which used to be called Drexel Boulevard, and stopped at a light. From all sides of the intersection, men descended on the truck. "Hey, Vic, what's the score?" said one. Another leaned in on my open window. "Thanks for that dresser. I picked it up from the alley the other day, good as new. What people throw out, it's crazy."

"Glad to hear," said Vic.

"Whatcha got today?"

"I need five guys ready to go until the job's done," said Vic. "Down on South Euclid. Here's the address." He passed a slip of paper with the number. "Oh, and we need a truck."

"No problem, boss," and the men dispersed.

"Lots of bosses," I said, as Vic turned and drove south and then east.

"The real boss is always the one with the purse strings," he said. "These guys like it when I come around because I pay better than anyone else. So I can count on them. Most of the pickers on the south side pay thirty dollars for a day of work. I pay one hundred dollars. But they have to come to do their share, otherwise I use someone else. The guy I was talking to sometimes works like a foreman."

After about ten minutes, we pulled up to a small midcentury house in a suburban enclave, a well-kept neighborhood with pockets of disused and abandoned property. He parked the truck out front. Five men, one of them the foreman, sat on the front porch, a fifteen-foot moving van parked in the driveway.

"What took you so long?" said one of them, flicking the butt of a cigarette onto the street.

Vic left me and made contact with the owner, who turned out to be Alton's ex-wife. She and some friends were already hauling garbage bags to the front of the driveway. "It's clothes," she told Vic. "We'll be working alongside you for the morning." While they negotiated and hammered out the finances of the day—I'd already figured out that Vic would get it going and coming, being paid by her for the salvage and by me for the stuff—I went down into the basement in back, where I was greeted by an elderly man. I introduced myself, and he told me he was Alton's ex-father-in-law.

"I remember when Alton brought Sonny around. He and his band would come to this house wearing all sorts of funny hats and capes. The neighbors were pretty wigged out." He paused, a portentous gatekeeper, and I thought about finding a glass of water to wash down a booster pill, my groin beginning to throb. "You figure this stuff's worth anything?"

"Yes, I expect it is," I said. "But I'm more interested in its meaning than its value. I think Sun Ra was brilliant. He should be as well known as Duke Ellington and Count Basie. And Alton was essential in helping push him out there. There's a lot of the story that hasn't been told."

"Sonny was about my age," he said, pushing himself from the folding chair he was sitting in to his feet. "Strange gentleman. OK, well, good luck with all that." He left, screen door banging after him.

Alone, I surveyed the room. A basement: tools, lawnmower, hose, and gloves, interspersed with piles of record covers, stacked face-up. *Omniverse in Blue. We Travel the Spaceways. Holiday for Soul Dance.* I picked up the top one on a stack, which was empty. Another, same, the back cover never tipped on, baring raw cardboard. I picked up a third one, and it had an LP inside. I checked, and the short stack of maybe thirty beneath it was full of records.

On a nearby workbench, there were tapes, reel-to-reel boxes covered with elaborate writing, some unspooling onto the floor. I made my way to a room toward the front of the house, the inside of which was a post-Katrinalike mess. Laying on top of one mound of papers was a larger rectangle of cardboard, a chunk taken out of the bottom corner, on which was a familiar image of a topless space woman arching backward over a moonscape. Weird, I thought, that someone would make so perfect a copy of the cover image of the second edition of *Jazz in Silhouette*. As luck would have it, an empty cover of the record was sitting on a shelf alongside several more. I held it next to the drawing, the comparison yielding to the fact that they were exactly the same; this was the original drawing for the cover. At that point, I knew we couldn't take anything for granted, no matter how disposable it looked.

Moving farther along into the rearmost room where the furnace was located, I noticed what looked like a kid's tent, an out-of-place piece of interior architecture. Four triangles of cardboard had been adjoined at the sides with tape, making a pyramid that peaked at the ceiling. There was just enough space along the bottom edge to crawl underneath, as if into a teepee. Inside were throw pillows and notebooks, some signed Bryant, some Abraham, and the remnants of similar lined sheets that had been burned. Candle drippings covered the floor. It was clearly a ritual spot. Pages in the books contained elaborate wish lists addressed: "Dear Creator, please grant me . . ." They were immodest. Cars, boats, fancy houses, and zillions of dollars were divined in these books, along with world peace, the eradication of hunger, and the power of flight.

"Oh, yeah, I forgot to tell you about this." Vic's voice startled me. "Crazy, isn't it? I wonder what they were up to."

"What's the story upstairs?"

"We're all set. There's one room over here," he walked me to a small padlocked interior space, "that they don't want us to take. Everything else is fair game."

I looked at the room. Tapes and stacks of posters and record covers filled it. Weeks later that room would be the source of nagging questions. Why that particular stuff and not the things they left out? What great wonders were in that room? Where did they go? Where are they now? In the heat of the moment I had no time for such speculation and simply plowed ahead.

"Cool, off limits, got it. Let's go."

I outlined my excavation priorities for Vic so he could pass them along to the guys. Tapes, sheet music, writings, drawings and record cover designs, instruments, Ra-related papers, PR material, relevant books. If we came across anything else that seemed possibly worthwhile... into the truck. We could sort it out later.

Box by box, we began moving things upstairs and onto the porch. I knew I shouldn't antagonize my wound, but I schlepped along with the others, stopping more frequently, but calculating that without my help we would never finish. There were surprises—the bottom layer of things in the front basement room had been through a flood, so it was moldy and rotten. We left it. One box of records, totally full, was crawling with bugs. It too was a casualty. Otherwise, up things went. Two 35-mm film canisters sat in a basement office, bearing a strip of white tape on the top: *Space Is The Place*. I took them to the front door and dropped them off, to be brought to the truck. A few minutes later Vic pulled me aside and said they didn't want us to take the film. "Fine, whatever they say, but let them know that we're not going to dig things out for them to choose between. They had months to sort."

Upstairs, we were working on different rooms, all of which were filled with variously fascinating material. At a certain point, midday, I noticed another crew seemed to be working with us. Sussing out their chief, I took a break. "Hi, I'm John." I said. "Who are you?"

"Name's Will," he said.

"What are you doing here?"

"I'm taking things away," he said. "I have a shop and I'll resell them."

I looked around at his guys, wondering what they thought about working with others doing the same thing and getting paid three times as much. "Who hired you?" I said.

"Vic invited me. Said there was too much for him, that I could have some."

"Well, I'm the one paying for all this stuff, so sorry to say, but please pack up this last load and head out."

A cheap golden sphinx statuette observed us from a bookcase, flanked by little copper pyramids.

"Hey, man. What's the deal with a white boy coming down here and taking all this important booty?" His voice changed, his inflection hardened. "You're raiding Tut's tomb, my friend, like those anthropologists. Raiding Tut's tomb!"

"What are you planning to do with the things you take? Putting them in a museum? Gonna drag 'em up to Du Sable and make good on your cultural patrimony?"

"Shut up, thief! This is my culture. I'll sell the shit out of it if I want to."

Vic interposed himself, and Will backed down, taking a bag of hats and hailing his men. "Not cool, Victor," he called over his shoulder.

"Why'd you call him?" I asked.

"Look, there's extra, so I thought I'd give him a taste."

"Triple dipping. So you wanted to be paid three ways!"

"You got a problem with getting paid?"

Over nine hours we uncovered a full truck's worth, topping off in the back of Vic's 4 by 4. A seeming piece of trash turned out to contain, when opened, what was labeled "El Saturn Treasure Map," laying out the global ambitions of Abraham and Bryant and, by association, Ra and the Arkestra. The world, according to this 1959 Ouiji board cartography, would soon be theirs. Notebooks and ledgers were all half full, abandoned at some unexceptional date; the full parts were fascinating, intimations of a business plan that included establishing a Cosmic Research Center and the acquisition of a limousine with proceeds from their million-selling singles. As a statement of purpose, it was so earnest and naive that one couldn't help but be smitten.

Alton had told me about their secret society, Thmei Research, and the dictionary of occult terms that they'd been working on for years. This item magically appeared, the list of participants with Ra's original name, Herman Poole Blount, charted in the colophon. Nearby were various Thmei artifacts: stationery, books, some documents. A few things didn't surface that afternoon, including any of Sun Ra's writings—the broadsides he'd allegedly written and distributed in the early years—and Ra's name-change document that Abraham had shown me in our first encounter, as he put it, "to prove I am who I say I am." About a year later, a cache of sixty or so of the broadsides turned up in one of the boxes; the Cook County government document escaped our efforts.

Vic's crew worked hard. Most of them were younger than me, in their thirties; friendly and quiet, they kept to their labor. One guy was much older. Maybe seventy-five, he was the most diligent of the men, hauling twice as much as the others; shirtless, he had the physique of a bodybuilder, chiseled and taut, with a frizzy beard and hair frosted bright white against his dark skin. He looked like someone had collaged an old man's head onto a twenty-five-year-old triathlete's body. The few times he spoke, it was through a nearly toothless mouth. In my mind, he conjured the biblical figure Ezekiel.

The foreman left all decisions to Vic, but he helped organize the trips up and down, making sure nobody went into the proscribed room, encouraging occasional breaks, managing the procurement of lunch. I took a break and sat on the cement steps out front. The surreal aura of the afternoon was setting in, and I reflected on what we were doing. From my perspective, this was an archive on a par with that of the most important literary figure or artist in American history, but a mysterious and very disorganized one—imagine if Ernest Hemingway's agent had been a hoarder, or if Willem de Kooning had been the head of a Masonic society whose papers were discovered ... in a blast zone.

The day resonated more personally, too. My relationship with Alton, our conversations about the stuff, even the specific objects—this had an air of unreality, a dream quality that was egged on by the painkillers and the way they subtly broke registration between what might happen and what was actually happening. As if through a veil, Alton's bass voice on the other end of the line: "Mr. Corbett, have you heard? The Germans bought a tape for one million dollars."

"Huh? What tape? What Germans?"

"I don't know exactly, but I have it from a reliable source."

"Whoever sold it must be a business genius; you could never recoup that much."

"Shows that the Germans are crazy for Sun Ra."

"Crazy would be the word."

I flashed to conversations with Ra himself, including one on his deathbed, his way of gliding between everyday reality and some unfamiliar kind of existence—another plane of there—in the span of a few words. We'd found the entire chain of production for the iconic cover of *Art Forms of Dimensions Tomorrow*, from Ra's own preliminary sketches, evolving over the course of several graph-paper pages in a notebook, through his refinements on onionskin paper and the addition of color, to the final ink drawing, the matching print plate, and finally test prints of the cover, which sports a flamboyantly curvaceous, cartoony outlay of his name with a jagged abstract drawing nested atop its central letters. The fact that all this might have gone into a landfill (where were the Germans now?), how tenuous all the connections were, the delete key, the rejected salvage, the fact that I was perhaps the only person Alton had told about the dictionary we'd just saved for posterity, the sheer amount of material that we were amassing and what the hell we would do with it. When I stopped to think about it, it was almost too much to fathom.

Work resumed, I snapped out of it and hauled and packed for the rest of the day. In a bundle of papers we found the original color separations, all hand-painted on vellum, for *Sun Ra Visits Planet Earth* and *Super-Sonic Jazz*. I made stacks of books, quickly selecting ones that dealt with music, mysticism, race, astronomy, astrology, history, and philosophy, sometimes flicking through them to try to identify Ra's permutation-filled marginalia. Manuals for obsolete typewriters, common medical books, how-to guides for home improvement—these were left. A copy of *Sex and the Single Girl* seemed relevant in its incongruousness. Some of the more unusual medical materials, including a selection of obscure machines, we took. Alton was one of the first African American X-ray technicians in Illinois, the fact of which is particularly interesting in light of his fascination with the occult and enlightenment: creating secret societies and making the unseen visible.

"Corbett, come down here!" Vic's voice resounded as the workday came near its finale. In the basement, there was a freestanding safe. "Should we crack it?" he asked, sensing the answer.

"I guess so," I said. A crowbar was procured, and all the workers gathered around, some pitching in, some watching while Vic and the foreman pried the ancient thing open like a squared-off giant clam. Seven of us crowded the unfinished room, empty but for a few books and stray pieces of timber, a broken accordion backed against a wall. With a clank, the safe's door came loose to reveal an empty shelf. Vic was panting, sweating profusely. A little cloud of dust rose from beneath the black metal box.

With one slow but smooth movement, the oldest worker reached down and strapped on the accordion. "Hey, there;' he said, tipping his grizzled head at my pajama bottoms and wheezing a few choked notes on the instrument. "You got the pants, now do the dance!"

Basking in the absurdity of the moment—where was I and what was I doing?—I did a wan little jig. But my crotch was shot, and I was beginning to fret over the next move. "I think we're done here," I said. "Vic, can we get to a phone?"

While the men finished packing and closing the truck, we drove to a pay phone, and I called home. My wife, Terri, had already been dealing with months of buildup to this, high anxiety and excitement and near obsession. She was the one who had at a much earlier point cautioned me against bankrupting myself—and, by proxy, her—with record shopping. But when she heard the tone in my voice, she knew it was serious.

"How much money do you have, in total?" I asked. She guessed, and I asked her to bring a check of hers, one of mine, and to get on the phone to find us a storage facility, preferably near where we lived, for a lot of stuff.

"What size storage?" she said.

"I don't know, exactly. It's a 15-foot truck and the back of Vic's pickup. Maybe 120 square feet?"

"Jeez," she said.

We swung back down to the house just as the gate closed on the moving van. Vic produced a beaten-up combination lock, passed out cash to everyone, and asked the foreman to meet us in a half hour at a Shell station on Cottage Grove. I thanked the guys as they one by one disappeared. Vic locked the front door and we pulled away, my head swimming.

Terri met us at the Foster-Ravenswood Storage, where she had procured two storage spaces, a big one, twelve by twelve feet, and another five by four. Ready for the day to be finished, we emptied the van first, sent the foreman on his way, then offloaded Vic's truck, the last of the items filling the bigger room to the grate that ceilinged it. Terri told me she had the checks, but together we didn't quite have enough money. I asked Vic if we could have a day or two. "I know where you live," he smirked.

That night I was tormented. My brain raced with the events of the day, images and words swirling together with perspiration and dust, a microburst of impressions. In the dark, we watched the Summer Olympics, swimmers and divers and runners doing their thing, breaking records or falling short. I had a fever. Changing my dressing was agony. And slowly a sinking feeling came over me. "Damn Sam," I said to my patient, comforting spouse. "We missed important things, I can feel it."

I phoned Vic and asked him to get us into the space again. He paused. It was very unlikely, he said, but if he could it would cost more. I told him fine, whatever it took. I slept restlessly, dream and drug and tension and elation mingling unhealthily.

Next morning, Vic told me we'd gotten the green light; we would have a few more hours in the house the next afternoon. After that, the new owners would take possession, and we'd be finished for real.

My rule of thumb, with repeat visits, if you've combed a collection or a store, is that they're generally unneeded. Intuition, sharp eyes, and the right frame of mind: one pass will suffice. You gather things in a state of autopilot, and like they say of car accidents, time extends to a point that you recognize the important things with near-flawless accuracy. Second-guess, go back for another survey, and you'll find the dregs, rarely anything that you would have chosen given all the time in the world.

That principle proved to be untrue in the case of the Alton Abraham archive. Vic and I once again drove southward, stopping for an early lunch at a soul food spot in a freestanding house. My recovery much advanced, narcotics downgraded to Tylenol, this time I wore pants—loose fitting, but slacks all the same. Vic knew half the restaurant's clients, animatedly greeting and being greeted, a table of two cops exchanging small talk with the celebrity picker. The waitress called him "Sugar" and gave us extra collards with our fried chicken, which, slathered in gravy, was divine.

At Alton's I immediately knew I had made the right call. A whole new room on the main floor seemed to have sprouted overnight, and inside there were more piles of posters and album cover materials. An air-conditioner box contained an Ampex reel-to-reel machine, possibly the one that Tommy "Bugs" Hunter had used to introduce on-the-fly tape-delay echo into Arkestra recordings, anticipating dub reggae by a decade. The forbidden room downstairs had been cleaned out, and the basement was basically empty. I took a roll of metallic filament from the workbench thinking it might be wire recordings; it turned out to be wire for fixing fences.

A huge walk-in wardrobe, which had been full of clothes two days earlier, was vacant except for a single black suit, hat, and white shoes—a tailor's apparition of Alton, which oversaw the final purge. Seeing the clothesless room, I realized one thing that I'd neglected to include in my priority list: costumes. As the story goes, Alton bought the Arkestra's first uniforms—anything but uniform—from a defunct opera company. I imagined the wigs and tricorner hats that Will may have taken, now for sale at a local junk store, the draping, sparkled, spangled garments hand embroidered by Ra, his beloved Buck Rogers caps with red flashing lights. No time for regrets, I thought, regretful nonetheless.

In the mounds of abandoned papers, which would have gone to the street along with everything else, I discovered the original documents for Ra's deal with ABC Impulse!, contracts which famously included the language that he and Alton crafted to cover extraterrestrial territories. Everywhere I looked, I discovered more tidbits. A scrap of Western Union receipt for a couple of dollars from Abraham to Ra, dated 1962. A little stack of unused tickets for a concert at Budland in 1956, sequentially numbered. The house fallen hollow and quiet, afternoon sun drew long and darkness settled on the day.

"Last call, Mr. Corbett." Vic's voice from the top of the stairs. "If you don't come up now, I'm leaving you here!"

I was on my hands and knees on the basement floor, pulling things from an overstuffed plastic garbage bag that sat alone in the middle of the room, readied for the curb. From the very bottom, I extracted a manila folder, inside of which were the original 1957 musician contracts for *Jazz in Silhouette*, the Arkestra's first LP on El Saturn, countersigned by all the players. John Gilmore and Pat Patrick's cursive handwriting looked alive in the underlined blank spaces. Tossing the folder on the small pile I'd erected, I took it all upstairs, joined Vic at his truck, and pulled the door locked behind me.

The next four years of my life were dedicated to the Abraham archive and research therein. It was an incredibly concentrated time, in parts frantic and a bit frightening for me. Far as I can tell, I came close to falling all the way down a well of compulsion. I could talk about little else. All conversation, no matter how it started, twined its way back to Sun Ra. I'm sure it was very boring, but I thought it was utterly captivating. I visited what we referred to as the "lockup" almost daily, brought things home to examine them more carefully, began the daunting task of sorting and cataloging, bought a working quarter-inch tape player and sampled tapes into the late hours, establishing a notebook which I decorated with "Sun Ra Archive—Tapes," in homage to Alton's enthusiastic annotations.

Retrospectively, Terri entertained a supernatural view of events: from the beyond, she figured, Ra and Abraham discussed the destiny of all the stuff, wracking their brains for someone who would be lunatic enough to shepherd and account for it all. "Remember that one guy? He's a total maniac," she'd say. "That was their conversation, just before you got the message. That e-mail didn't come from Mike Watt, it came from Sonny and Alton."

The piles still settling, Terri and I established a circle of advisers, people whose opinions, judgment, and ethics we trusted. We were judicious with whom and how much we divulged, in part out of a well-founded fear that Ra fanatics would hound us. The first week, distant acquaintances of Heather's e-mailed me, telling me they'd seen Ra in the '70s and just loved him. "All we want is a souvenir, something to feel closer to him." Hamza Walker, our old friend and a curator at the Renaissance Society, visited the lock-up at a preliminary point, taking photos and discussing a possible show. I'd already imagined an extensive exhibition. Hamza floated it by Susanne Ghez, the Ren's director; she was unconvinced that it made sense for the institution, which exclusively showed work by living artists. At a music conference at Wesleyan, I told trombonist and scholar George Lewis about the archive; he was enthusiastic and supportive, and he urged me to start writing about it. Rachel Weiss, head of arts administration at the School of the Art

Institute of Chicago, and Anthony Elms, independent curator and publisher of White Walls, both made trips to the lock-up in the first months, and they helped us think about the future of the materials. Jazz journalist Kevin Whitehead assisted as we began to collate the disparate material, segregating things into labeled boxes. Independently, I told music writers Lloyd Sachs and Peter Margasak about it; they both sat listening to the story, jaws slackened.

Stimulated by the notion of an exhibition, we contacted the Smart Museum, on the campus of the University of Chicago. Curators Stephanie Smith and Richard Born visited our apartment, looking through some of the prize pieces; ultimately, they decided not to do the show because it would all be coming from a single set of owners, a move frowned upon curatorially. Anthony and I discussed the notion of a show at the Hyde Park Art Center (HPAC). A proposal was tendered, and HPAC agreed, contingent on Elms joining the curatorial team, which would consist of me, Terri, and him. Around that time, we discovered Sun Ra's incredible early writings, a sensationally robust group of them, typewritten by Ra, some carbon-copied, others in manuscript form complete with his penciled marginalia. Anthony suggested producing a facsimile edition, which was published a few years later, just before the HPAC exhibition.

As much as I felt the free fall of fascination, I was simultaneously experiencing an identity crisis. On one hand, the material was rich and generative; as George foresaw, I was intent on digging in and initiating some literature on it, in hopes of others jumping in. But the vinyl freak side of my personality was experiencing its own libidinal glee: "Holy crap, I own all of this!" I fussed over which of the cover designs we would frame and hang at home, and fantasized over what incredible material might be hiding on the reels. Years of stalking record stores in search of any El Saturns, excitement over the occasional ABC Impulse! acquisition, also the rare ones nabbed from friends, ex-freaks who were selling their collections, including *Strange Strings* and the elusive *When Angels Speak of Love*. But what would happen to a freak if all his freakish desires were answered, more than he could imagine? Those past triumphs seemed trivial, mundane. This was the mother lode. I had been to the promised land. Be careful what you wish for ... it might just crush you.

Terri, ever wiser than I, discussed these unfamiliar feelings with me. "You know, there's such thing as too much happiness. It's not good for you to be too excited all the time." This thought had never occurred to me, raised in a conventional pleasure-seeking household. "Happiness and excitement can be attachments." I recognized a Buddhist line of thought. "It seems to me that with all these things, you've gotten everything you could ever want, and now you're becoming too attached to them. We don't really own anything. You can't take it with you."

About three years into this phase, an acquaintance named Jim Dempsey called me about introducing a series of Sun Ra films at the theater he managed. I invited him to the lock-up, and we devised a small show of photographs in the lobby during a month of screenings, the first public light seen by the archive. Terri, Anthony, and I readied the stuff for the book and the show. Then, after about four years, I had completely exhausted myself and had to step away. By that time, Rachel had asked me to serve as chair of Exhibition Studies, a program in Arts Admin, and Jim and I, inspired by the fun of the film center's Sun Ra Sundays, had convinced ourselves that we should open an art gallery. My hands full, I had plenty of reason to back off the archive a bit.

Something changed inside me over the next two years. I found the notion of going record hunting slightly absurd—what could ever top the two days in the Alton house? And Terri's words rang true: we didn't own any of it, we were stewards, keepers, hyper-specialized salvagers. We continued paying to store everything, though we were living more or less hand to mouth. Inventorying and caring for everything was beginning to seem like a burden, more than a joy, although there was still something spine-tinglingly unreal about it. Sorting stuff meant tossing inessentials—candy wrappers, mouse poop, newspapers from 1982, an inoperative Luger pistol, Alton's gun license, some live bullets, anything personal of his that we found. Even weeding out we were only able to trim away the smaller of the two spaces. The large one remained full to bursting, big aluminum door roaring open every time I visited, the oversweet odor of unburnt incense from another locker wafting together with other normal storage facility smells of mildew, off-gassing mattresses, and decaying cardboard.

When *Pathways to Unknown Worlds: Sun Ra, El Saturn & Chicago's Afro-Futurist Underground, 1954–68* opened at HPAC in October 2006, Terri and I had a plan. In one of the interviews about the show with a local paper, I dropped a hint that we were looking for an institutional home for the archive. We were inspired, as well, by a phone correspondence that turned into a friendship with Adam Abraham, Alton's son, who called HPAC a few weeks before the exhibition opened, having scouted it online. Adam's response to hearing the saga: he was disappointed he couldn't have been there to help save all his dad's material, life had intervened, but he was pleased and thankful that we had, particularly that we were keeping it intact, and he was excited about the prospect of it finding a proper permanent residence.

Not long after the night of the reception, which was packed with visitors, we were contacted by Deborah Gillaspie, head of the Chicago Jazz Archives in Special Collections at the University of Chicago's Regenstein Library. The three of us met for dinner, and Deborah asked us what we thought of the Alton material going to U. of C. Handshakes over dessert. Like that, we had a new place for the stuff, fulfilling our dream of it staying on the South Side, in a facility with ample resources, accessible to the general public and to scholars as well. Our negotiations over the following year included a few stipulations. They could have anything they wanted, but anything they left was ours to do with as we wanted. In perpetuity, we could use any of the materials that we could obtain rights for, and if anyone else was going to use it, they had to ask permission through us. The tapes would go to another archive; Special Collections did not have proper facilities to manage sound recordings. And we had been working on traveling the HPAC show, so we needed to be sure we could carry through on that.

My friend Lou Mallozzi was founder and director of the Experimental Sound Studio (ESS), where I often did remastering in preparation for releases on the Unheard Music series. I'd worked on some of the Ra tapes there, too, though the ever-jovial John McCortney at Air Wave Studios had given me such a ridiculous rate for transferring that he and I digitized about fifty of the four hundred tapes, breathlessly waiting to hear what would come next as the tape randomly changed speed and format. A few tapes into it, we figured out that they would sometimes hide things at the out tail of a reel, a two-minute song camouflaged like a snake rolled up in a garden hose.

Over espresso at our favorite bakery one afternoon, I proposed to Lou that the world needed a sound-specific archive designed to save some of the imperiled tapes that were being orphaned as their caretakers died, lost interest, or were otherwise disinvested. As an example, I suggested the El Saturn tapes, which hadn't gone to the University of Chicago. After months of consideration, he agreed and inaugurated the Creative Audio Archive (CAA); the Abraham tapes and Michael Zerang's Links Hall archive constituted a hearty first two batches.

Pathways traveled to the Institute of Contemporary Art, Philadelphia, in 2010, where it received a glowing full-page *New York Times* review. Anthony published a couple more books: a catalog of the show and a compendium of the symposium that we'd organized in Chicago, the latter containing more unpublished images from the archive. A few years hence, direct quotations from the Ra broadsides cropped up in several visual artists' work. In 2013, the Studio Museum in Harlem featured Ra as a source of Afro-

Futurism in *The Shadows Took Shape,* and it is now less uncommon to hear him discussed among artists as a major inspiration, perhaps due in some part to the dissemination of the Alton materials. The audio archive, dutifully and lovingly transferred to listenable digital format by a small cadre of engineers including Todd Carter, has been inventoried complete on the CAA website. Appointments are made to come listen to any of it, and through a commission program at ESS, young musicians and sound artists have put the previously unknown recordings into active service.

Meanwhile, a weight had been lifted from me. Not only in terms of the Alton material, also the vinyl urgency, a habit that had been transformed into something more reasonable, a trickle not a torrent. Nine months after salvaging the house, Vic called to say another picker had sold him some Sun Ra books that he'd found by the side of the road, things that had been discarded before we got there. I bought them from him, six copies of *Extensions Out: The Immeasurable Equation Vol. 2,* Ra's second book of collected poetry. It was a title that I'd never seen, an extreme rarity. We gave the library a couple of them, kept the others, along with plenty of multiples and posters, ones that they only wanted in a few copies for their collection. Much of the Alton–Ra book collection was deemed too moldy for the Regenstein, and we hung onto it. The artist Cauleen Smith later used the books for an installation.

Though we still had lots of Ra ephemera, a couple of years after we gave everything to the two institutions, I experienced a bout of what could only be called donor's remorse.

"Why didn't I just keep one of the original record cover designs?" I whined to myself.

It wasn't a month later that I was looking through my flat files, inventorying record covers that the library had left us. Shuffling though sheets of silver foil prints, I noticed one that didn't look exactly like the others, its image applied directly onto the blank silver record cover. I looked closely. It was drawn, not printed. Sun Ra's original mock-up for *Other Planes of There.* One final wish granted with a wink to a freak from out there in those other planes. Wherever Sun Ra and Alton Abraham now reside.

Sites of Formation 1972

FOUR THOUGHTS ABOUT MILES DAVIS'S *ON THE CORNER*

Chris Pitsiokos

FAILED ATTEMPTS AT SELLING OUT ARE THE BEST

Miles Davis wasn't quiet about his intentions to broaden his audience. In his *Autobiography* he says, "It was with *On the Corner* and *Big Fun* that I really made an effort to get my music over to young black people. They are the ones who buy records and come to concerts, and I had started thinking about building a new audience for the future."[1] Apart from employing Stevie Wonder/Motown bassist Michael Henderson, Miles included more funk and R&B elements in *On the Corner* than he had ever before, citing Sly Stone and James Brown among his popular music influences. The sounds of popular music permeate the album, from Henderson's stripped-down bass grooves to Davis's use of wah-wah trumpet. The use of handclaps on *Black Satin* is reminiscent of Sly Stone's use of claps in *Stand!*, especially on the track "I Want to Take You Higher," as pointed out to me by multi-instrumentalist, composer, and *On the Corner* fan Tyshawn Sorey.

Far from quickly expanding his audience, *On the Corner* was a commercial failure. Davis felt that this had to do with Columbia's refusal to market the recording as a pop album.[2] He may have had a point.

Regardless of the reason, *On the Corner*, initially, was almost universally maligned. Mainstream jazz and rock critics, esteemed avant-garde musicians, and even some of the musicians on the recording initially disliked the music. Eugene Chadbourne, in an article for *CODA*, wrote, "His new music is pure arrogance. It's like coming home and finding Miles there, his fancy feet up on your favorite chair"[3]; Paul Buckmaster, who provided arrangements and plays electric cello on the album said, "It was my least favorite Miles album"; and Dave Liebman, who plays the first solo on the album explained, "I didn't think much of it."[4]

In time, the rock and pop community, and later, some subsets of the jazz community, would come around. Rock critic Lester Bangs, who initially hated the album, came to consider it a masterpiece that captured the sound of the modern metropolis.[5] Paul Buckmaster would ultimately praise the album in the liner notes to *The Complete On the Corner Sessions* box set.[6] *On the Corner*'s influence today is incalculable.

Incidentally, the other great electric free funk band of the 1970s, Ornette Coleman's Prime Time, was also an ill-fated attempt at expanding an audience. Coleman missed the immediate connection he had with the audience in the rhythm-and-blues bands he played in in his youth. His experience with the Master Musicians of Jajouka inspired him to try to renew that connection while maintaining his dedication to creative, forward-thinking art music.

He believed he could attain this through the introduction of rock rhythms and electric guitars.[7]

Both Davis and Coleman's incorporations of popular idioms completely failed to capture the audience that they desired, but their attempts resulted in some of the most challenging, strange, hybridic, futuristic music of the second half of the 20th century.

HYBRIDIC MUSIC

Paul [Buckmaster] was into Bach and so I started paying attention to Bach while Paul was around. I had begun to realize that some of the things Ornette Coleman had said about things being played three or four ways, independently of each other were true because Bach had also composed that way. What I was playing on On the Corner *has no label, although people thought it was funk because they didn't know what else to call it. It was actually a combination of some of the concepts of Paul Buckmaster, Sly Stone, James Brown, and Stockhausen, some of the concepts I had absorbed from Ornette's music, as well as my own.*[8]
- Miles Davis

'nuff said.

STOCKHAUSEN

Paul Buckmaster met Miles Davis in 1969 when Davis was performing in London. Davis was impressed by a Buckmaster track he heard and the two became friends. In April 1972 Davis invited Buckmaster to come to New York to help him work on a new recording. Buckmaster arrived in New York shortly thereafter and moved into Davis's house for a few months, sleeping on his couch. He brought a record by German composer Karlheinz Stockhausen that included the pieces *Gruppen*, a piece for 109 musicians divided into three groups, and one of the earliest works for orchestra and live electronics, *Mixtur*. Davis, who had a sound system that ran throughout his house, blared *Gruppen* and *Mixtur* for several days. He also purchased a cassette of another Stockhausen piece, *Hymnen*, that he kept in his Lamborghini.[9] *Hymnen* is an electronic work that includes recordings of national anthems from several countries, with the option of adding live performers. *On the Corner* was recorded less than two months after Davis's first brush with Stockhausen's music, and yet he cites it as an influence—one heard in both the expansion of his electronic vocabulary, and his compositional methodology.

It turns out the inspiration was mutual. Possibly encouraged by his son Markus, who is a trumpet player, Stockhausen became increasingly interested when Davis went electric. The influence is apparent in Stockhausen's composition *Ceylon/Bird of Passage*, released in 1975, which uses electric/wah-wah trumpet, bird whistle, synthesizer, and Kandyan drum, among other instruments. The instrumentation is quite similar to *On the Corner*, especially the end of "Black Satin," which includes bird whistle, electric wah-wah trumpet, synthesizer, and tabla (similar to Kandyan drum).[10] Like *On the Corner, Ceylon/Bird of Passage* was a strange crossover and was critically maligned. Its lack of success was also largely driven by how it was marketed—in the world of rock, rather than contemporary classical.

Davis and Stockhausen would finally meet in June of 1980 in Columbia Studios. The result of this collaboration is still unissued.[11] (Dear God, please let this see the light of day!)

COLOTOMIC JAMS

Notwithstanding my distaste for modern bands that accept the "jam band" epithet, the *On the Corner* band is definitively a "jam band": a static or minutely changing groove is indefatigably asserted by the bass and drums, while most of the rest of the band comps or improvises. Davis reportedly instructed bassist Michael Henderson to not follow the other members of the band "out."

Yet the band's approach subverts not only jam band *modus operandi*, but also that of Western Music in general. Avoiding the Western musical trope of the simulated orgasm (e.g.: dominant/tonic, tension/release, crescendo/decrescendo) *On the Corner* is an "all-over" piece, much like the work of some abstract expressionists. There is no single focal point. Rather than listening forward or backwards to the climax, the listener must focus on the ever-present *now* (this was an important tenet of Ornette Coleman's music as well). While musicians enter and exit, the music slowly evolves, even though homeostasis is maintained throughout. The only hard transitions on the recording were made after the fact, by Teo Macero cutting and pasting tape (on *Black Satin*, for instance).

One of the ways Davis achieves this "all-over" effect is by stratifying the rhythm and the rates of change within the band. Colotomy is the term used to describe the nested rhythmic cycles used in gamelan music. In colotomy, a specific instrument is used to demarcate a specific time interval. The instruments are stratified, so one instrument will demarcate a very long time interval, another will demarcate a subdivision of that long time interval, a third instrument will demarcate an even smaller subdivision, and so on.

On the Corner uses a similar strategy. For instance, at the beginning of the title track, the bass is demarcating every four beats, the cowbell every two beats, the guitar every beat (on the up-beat), and the tabla every sixteenth note (quarter of a beat). Therefore, we are hearing the rhythm in at least four levels, each representing a different subdivision of the measure or rhythmic cycle.

Davis's approach goes beyond simple time demarcation, however. The levels of the ensemble have different rates of improvisational change in their playing. While the bassist changes very slowly, adding and taking away approach notes throughout the duration of a long jam, the guitarist changes at a faster rate. The keyboardists seem to take a middle road and the soloist, of course, changes at the fastest rate. What we are hearing is a stratified approach to rates of change in improvisation: this stratification is expressed not only in demarcations of time in colotomic cycles, but in the rates of change by each of the members of the band. Some members change extremely slowly, reacting to the longtime energetic changes of the ensemble; some are hyper-reactive, moment to moment; others are somewhere in between. Of course, some of the players are able to occupy different strata at different moments of the piece (for instance when the guitar moves from being a rhythm section instrument to a solo instrument). Miles Davis explains his thoughts behind this in his *Autobiography*:

> *Through Stockhausen I understood music as a process of elimination and addition. Like 'yes' only means something after you have said 'no.' I was experimenting a lot, for example, telling a band to play rhythm and hold it and not react to what was going on; let me do the reacting.*[12]

Works Cited

Bergstein, Barry: "Miles Davis and Karlheinz Stockhausen: A Reciprocal Relationship." In *The Musical Quarterly*, Volume 76, No. 4 (Winter, 1992). Oxford University Press, 502–525.

Buckmaster, Paul: *The Complete On the Corner Sessions*, liner notes. Columbia C6K 06239, 2007.

Davis, Miles (with Quincy Troupe). *Miles: The Autobiography*. New York: Simon & Schuster Paperbacks, 1989.

Freeman, Philip. *Running the Voodoo Down: The Electric Music of Miles Davis*. San Francisco: Backbeat Books, 2005.

Litweiler, John. *Ornette Coleman: A Harmolodic Life*. New York: William Morrow & Co., 1993.

Silverman, Jack: "Jazz saxophonist Dave Liebman comes to Nashville to revisit Miles Davis's explosive and polarizing *On the Corner*." In *Nashville Scene*, 2015. https://www.nashvillescene.com/music/article/13057913/jazz-saxophonist-dave-liebman-comes-to-nashville-to-revisit-miles-davis-explosive-and-polarizing-on-the-corner

Tingen, Paul: "The most hated album in jazz." In *The Guardian*, 2007. https://www.theguardian.com/music/2007/oct/26/jazz.shopping

1   Davis, Miles (with Quincy Troupe). *Miles: The Autobiography*. New York: Simon & Schuster Paperbacks, 1989, 324.
2   Davis, Miles (with Quincy Troupe). *Miles: The Autobiography*. New York: Simon & Schuster Paperbacks, 1989, 328.
3   Quoted in: Silverman, Jack: "Jazz saxophonist Dave Liebman comes to Nashville to revisit Miles Davis's explosive and polarizing *On the Corner*." In *Nashville Scene*, 2015. https://www.nashvillescene.com/music/article/13057913/jazz-saxophonist-dave-liebman-comes-to-nashville-to-revisit-miles-davis-explosive-and-polarizing-on-the-corner
4   Quoted in: Tingen, Paul: "The most hated album in jazz." In *The Guardian*, 2007. https://www.theguardian.com/music/2007/oct/26/jazz.shopping
5   Freeman, Philip. *Running the Voodoo Down: The Electric Music of Miles Davis*. San Francisco: Backbeat Books, 2005, 98.
6   Buckmaster, Paul: *The Complete On the Corner Sessions*, liner notes. Columbia C6K 06239, 2007, 71–79.
7   Litweiler, John. *Ornette Coleman: A Harmolodic Life*. New York: William Morrow & Co., 1993, 158.
8   Davis, Miles (with Quincy Troupe). *Miles: The Autobiography*. New York: Simon & Schuster Paperbacks, 1989, 322
9   Buckmaster, Paul: *The Complete On the Corner Sessions*, liner notes. Columbia C6K 06239, 2007, 61–64.
10 Bergstein, Barry: "Miles Davis and Karlheinz Stockhausen: A Reciprocal Relationship." In *The Musical Quarterly*, Volume 76, No. 4 (Winter, 1992). Oxford University Press, 514.
11 Bergstein, Barry: "Miles Davis and Karlheinz Stockhausen: A Reciprocal Relationship." In *The Musical Quarterly*, Volume 76, No. 4 (Winter, 1992). Oxford University Press, 502.
12 Davis, Miles (with Quincy Troupe). *Miles: The Autobiography*. New York: Simon & Schuster Paperbacks, 1989, 329.

DEREK BAILEY'S *ON THE EDGE: IMPROVISATION IN MUSIC*

Peter Margasak

In September of 1987 I went to see a solo concert by Derek Bailey in Chicago, part of a series at the space Links Hall curated by percussionist Michael Zerang. I was 20 at the time, and I probably had one or two records by the British guitarist, but I certainly hadn't invested a lot of time in them and my ears hadn't experienced much free improvisation yet. I just knew that he was important, somehow. The performance confused me, and I was unable to engage in what he was doing in any meaningful way. The experience had a profound impact on me, as it does whenever some alien strain of music leaves me puzzled or angered. It stayed with me, needling me to dig into it, to understand it, and place it in a wider context.

The more I learned about Bailey the more complex his conceptions became—even though, in essence, they were all quite simple. Bailey's skepticism for working improvisational bands, for example, perplexed me. I only considered the upside of how a unit like the Schlippenbach Trio or AMM could develop its peculiar language and approach over time, its members telepathically anticipating one another's moves. I was also stymied by how a guy who dismissed recordings of improvised music simultaneously ran Incus Records, one of the most prolific and best labels dedicated to the discipline. The idea of improvisation as a life practice[1] was far too abstruse for this twentysomething to understand, so Bailey's commitment to perpetually put himself out on a limb—embracing that condition as his life force—all seemed impossibly abstract to me back then. Yet ultimately, that mindset defined his life and work—a process approach at odds with any sort of music industry.

It would be years before I picked up a copy of his essential book, *Improvisation: Its Nature and Practice in Music*, which was originally published in 1980. I'm sure I didn't get around to actually reading it until after the BBC's Channel 4 produced and aired a four-part television program called *On the Edge: Improvisation in Music* in 1992. Bailey wrote and narrated the series—which was directed by award-winning music documentarian Jeremy Marre—based on the research he conducted for his book. I wouldn't see it until more than a decade after it was made. A revised version of the book was published around the same time, augmented with material from the interviews Bailey conducted for the TV program. It's mind-boggling that this documentary hasn't been made available commercially—although it's easy enough to find crude VHS transfers of the show over at UbuWeb—because decades later there still isn't a better or more accessible introduction to the concept of improvisation in the broadest possible terms, even if Bailey's inclusions are subjective and anything but comprehensive. Of course, researching improvisation was a peculiar project for him, not his life's work.

While the guitarist privileged the practice of free improvisation in his book, devoting much of it to reflecting on his own experiences with the Joseph Holbrooke Trio (Gavin Bryars and Tony Oxley), Music Improvisation Company (Evan Parker, Jamie Muir, Christine Jeffrey, and Hugh Davies), Company Weeks (ad hoc gatherings he organized between 1987 and 1994 with a cast of improvisers that increasingly included practitioners from disparate traditions and disciplines) and countless other interactions with the diverse array of players who emerged from the British scene, the documentary is more balanced. In both the book and the documentary Bailey eschews hierarchies, instead examining traditions as diverse as Indian classical music, liturgical organ music, qawwali, flamenco, bluegrass, classic Andalusian music, salsa, the Grateful Dead (not exactly a "tradition" but certainly distinct from most other rock bands), electric blues, Gaelic psalm singing, and western classical music, pulling together threads from each to support his contention that improvisation is a central element of all of them, or at least to their development.

The fact that the first episode opens in Chicago, with AACM reedist Douglas Ewart leading a workshop in a Chinatown elementary school, encouraging a diverse mix of kids through guided improvisation to explore it on their own individual terms, makes clear that Bailey's passion for the practice isn't rooted in any specific style or school of thought, an idea reinforced as the series unfolds. Again, improvisation was far more than a style or school of thought for the guitarist—it was the way he lived his life. In his book he spends several pages looking into the educational methodologies of percussionist John Stevens of Spontaneous Music Ensemble, who embraced a vaguely similar openness and spirit of generosity in spreading the practice of free improvisation.

The program ends with a non-judgmental segment on New York hip-hop, considering the improvisational elements at play in the scratching of a DJ, ironic given Bailey's cantankerous attitude toward music designed as entertainment. (Despite his famous antipathy toward pop music, Bailey wasn't afraid of technological developments in music, which led him to collaborate with various electronic music producers, such as Chicagoans like Casey Rice, Bundy K. Brown, and John Herndon, who provided tracks for him to tussle with for the 1999 album *Playbacks*. Witnessing a live performance with Rice in Chicago in 2001 only increased my admiration of Bailey's utter fearlessness and his ability to cut to the core of any encounter.)

Compared to the book, where Bailey tends to express a more critical mindset—dismissing hard bop altogether—he tends to moderate his position in the documentary, although that doesn't stop him from saying of European classical music: "To invent something is totally beyond the scope of the modern orchestra. Its function seems to be more, ahem, technological or, at best, Pavlovian. And, perhaps, they get nearest to improvisation when they're tuning up." In contrast, he offers an extended scene with pianist Robert Levin, who celebrates the fact that most great composers were also working musicians, and some of the most lionized works built in space for improvisation—a practice banished by standardization enforced by the record industry and the expectations of audiences demanding "perfect" readings of a piece they've internalized.

In a feature published in the *Wire* in 2004, a little more than a year before Bailey passed away, author David Keenan writes, "Bailey now believes that free improvisation itself has become so codified and defined that it's effectively neutered, its many recordings serving to fix musical identities and establish operative tropes while labels, promoters, and festivals unwittingly collude to provide a superstructure that facilitates career improvisers and assorted specialists." From the same feature, Bailey: "'I think improvisation's great era is over, its time is gone,' he sighs. 'My impression is that for any music to be really vibrant it lasts about seven or eight years. That's all of music, every music period. Bebop, Dixie, whatever, there's a vibrant period that lasts seven or eight years and after that, it's over.'"

Indeed, toward the end of his own book, the guitarist writes, "One of a variety of reasons that led me in 1974 to start putting this book together was a suspicion that freely improvised music as an identifiable separate music was finished. Like some early 20th-century 'ism,' I vaguely felt, it had run its course and would probably continue to exist, if at all, only as some kind of generalized influence." While he then goes on to express enthusiasm for new strains of improvisation that developed in the mid-'70s, citing the British quartet Alterations, which deployed ideas from popular and non-Western music into its collective improvisations, it's hardly a secret that Bailey was no Pollyanna or thoughtless cheerleader.

In the documentary, the guitarist embraces new modes of organized free improvisation, whether John Zorn's game piece *Cobra*, the conductions of Lawrence "Butch" Morris, George Lewis's interactive computer programs, or new tweaks on hallowed traditional forms, such as the open forms of the Korean kayagum master Sang-Won Park and the chaotic humor in Eugene Chadbourne's disemboweling of country and western. I think it's telling that most of the final half of the last episode digs into traditional sounds and rituals of Zimbabwe's Shona people, reinforcing the way improvisational practices lie at the root of all music-making. After spending hours illustrating diverse contemporary manifestations of improvisation, this drives home one of his final points, exploring it in a non-abstract, everyday form where its characteristics haven't been transformed into ornamental dressing.

In Bailey's book, composer Earle Brown seems relatively sanguine about the role of the practice in composed music. "I believe affirmatively that improvisation is a musical art which passed out of Western usage for a time but it is certainly back now," he says. "And I felt that it would come back, which is why I based a lot of my work on certain aspects of it. It's here and I think it's going to stay. And it's not going to do away with the writing of music but it's going to bring an added dimension—of aliveness—to a composition and bring the musician into a greater intensity of working on that piece."

Indeed, when Bailey wrote the book it was incredibly rare to find musicians who worked with composed materials and who could also improvise, apart from Levin whose practice fit into the tradition of Bach or Mozart, or the liturgical organ players (represented in the documentary by Naji Hakim). He does include several such players, including the classical clarinetist Antony Pay, who describes improvisations he played while recording music by Stockhausen and who would eventually take part in Bailey's Company gatherings, as well as violinist Alexander Bălănescu. In general, however, Bailey doesn't share Brown's optimism. I'd say Brown has turned out to be more prescient, as the growth of musicians equally fluent in free improvisation and composed music—whether jazz-based, experimental, or classical musicians—has rapidly expanded in the decades since Bailey completed his project. The role of improvisation in notated art or experimental music has arguably become more ubiquitous and advanced in the last couple of decades than it has in centuries.

Of course, this development doesn't necessarily support Bailey's devotion to improvisation. Indeed, many of these new manifestations relegate improvisation as an element or feature, and not a way of making music. As Bailey wrote in the book, "In all its roles and appearances, improvisation can be considered as the celebration of the moment. And in this nature improvisation exactly resembles the nature of music. Essentially, music is fleeting; its reality is its moment of performance. There might be documents that relate to that moment—score, recording, echo, memory—but only to anticipate it or recall it." To the generations that came to this music through recordings,[2] that insistence might seem quaint or wrong-headed but it sums up Bailey's commitment to exploration and spontaneity, above all else, and that spirit comes through *On the Edge* nearly three decades after it was made. If the Internet has made Bailey's catholic inclusions less impressive, nothing has weakened or made his salient observations less powerful or important.

1   In my reading, Bailey never spent much time discussing his embrace of improvisation as life force, but he nevertheless seems to have lived it. But I'd be remiss if I didn't mention George Lewis, who has written and lectured extensively on the idea. http://www.hemi.nyu.edu/journal/4.2/eng/en42_pg_lewis.html

2   The David Grubbs book *Records Ruin the Landscape* (Duke) spends a great deal of space examining how pioneers of experimental music felt antipathy towards recordings of their work, while subsequent generations could experience much of that work only through recordings.

SOCIAL OR MUTUAL AID MUSIC

Nate Wooley

Sites of Formation (SoF) has been a recurring feature in *Sound American* since Issue 21 and was intended to provide an editorial framework upon which our contributors can propose topics that may not fit into that issue's central theme. Each set of *SoF*s is generated by year multiples based on the issue number. For example, *SA21* featured articles based on the years using multiples of 21: 1921, 1942, 1963, 1984, and 2005. The writers can propose any topic related to the year, such as an important composition being premiered, a seminal recording being released, a musical figure's birth or death, or, in the best circumstances, some completely odd idea that the year triggers in their mind. This concept, like many that I've come up with for *SA* since its inception, is shaggy and cumbersome, and I like it that way. Although it may mean some difficulty for myself and *SA*'s contributors to portion out the essays based on such an arbitrary system, I have found that it this kind of awkwardness has great potential for spawning wonderful new ideas.

This issue, *SA24*, is the first to mathematically push the *SoF* concept into the future/present, as one of its possible years is 2020, the year for which this issue is the first of three, creating a particularly awkward situation. How does one tease out a topic from the events of a year that has only just begun (three weeks in as of this writing). A lot *has* happened, so it is conceivable that an enterprising young writer could rely on those three weeks of information to come up with a fine bit of sartorial music writing. Unfortunately, no such writer stepped forward, so you get a semi-worn out and middle-aged editor in their place.

Instead of combing the events of early 2020 for inspiration or dwelling in the present and writing a state-of-the-music speech—a task I neither deserve nor want to do, I've decided to use the opportunity of *Sites of Formation* 2020 to look to the future and write a gentle manifesto of making music *together*. Time will tell whether I, or you, remain interested in the ideas presented below, but that's what makes writing about the present so satisfying; it is always true to its ideas at the time that they are written.

All art relies on a relationship to complexity. Confining ourselves to music, a composition or performance, an idea, or a musical personality is, at least partially, measured—positively or negatively—by our reaction to its complexity. A piece by Elliott Carter, Gérard Grisey, Pauline Oliveros, Roscoe Mitchell, Éliane Radigue can all be broken down and given a qualitative description based solely on how we encounter its intricacy, depth, or density. Carter's music is one in which the complexity is explicit as an intricacy and density of architecture, notation, and sound. Grisey's may move to the more implicit as a certain extra-musical knowledge of the physics of sound and depth of listening is presupposed. Oliveros's music may vary by performance, but the weight of her concepts supplies a kind of indeterminacy as complexity. And, on the other side of that dialectic, Mitchell's music is built somewhat off of an improvisation in the same way. Éliane Radigue's music is often seen as simple or minimalist, a drone, but as those who have developed a deep relationship to the sound of her compositions can attest, the sheer weight of the micro-events occurring within a minimal amount of pitches is as intricate and dense as any Boulez work.

The reader may disagree with any or all of these characterizations, but to do so they must engage on some level with complexity, which only solidifies the position. And, suffice it to say, all of the above examples contain valid ways of generating complex work. These forms of complexity will continue to be valid historically and will morph into new forms over time. However, I would like to make a case here for a deeper exploration of a less-used complexity that is based on human interaction, communication, and community. The way in which material is produced and articulated, either spontaneously or through pre-planning, is qualitatively different when it is produced by two or more people communicating with each other toward a common goal of making music that transcends their individual performance.

That is an especially fiddly definition of what I'm after but for good reason, as the first thing that comes to most people's minds when I bring up this idea of, what I call, "mutual aid" complexity or social music is that it already exists in jazz improvisation or in experimental music concepts of indeterminacy. However, there are some basic reasons why I believe this way of thinking to be something set apart from either of those two forms.

In jazz or freely improvised music, a language is presupposed and codified within each player's history and aesthetic. In the best cases, this language can be molded to fit into a group sound, creating something more transcendent than a variation on the sound of single or multiple, simultaneous, soloists. More often than not, however, the end result is multiple individual languages being spoken at the same time; not uninteresting, but a different quality of complexity.

Indeterminacy, on the other hand, asks the performers to subvert their personal language in order to take on the composer's aesthetic and language by asking them to work within the preset parameters proposed by that composer or, as often is the case now, the legacy and cultural detritus set up around the memory of that composer. Again, valid and interesting as a way of building a kind of complexity, but producing an altogether different qualitative result.

Beyond improvisation and indeterminacy, I believe there are modes of working that emphasize the act of collective decision making over personal narrative or an imposed structure. Elements of both remain present, of course, as performers will always have a sense of musical self and material for any sort of compositional activity has to come from somewhere. But, by structuring a piece of music so that the material was structured to provoke conversation, process, and unity amongst the musicians by asking them to collectively *choose* what parts of their language is best suited to the creation of a mutually beneficial outcome, it creates a situation in which the profound complexity of the human to be celebrated in musical form.

In other words, improvisation and indeterminacy deal primarily with the vocabulary of either a performer or composer, and what I'm proposing is composition as a basic set of syntactical rules in order to allow musicians the flexibility to create collective poetry. This way of composing would allow musicians to access the full breadth of their musical history without defaulting to a bricolage of genres. A group of musicians and composers working on how they can, as a unit, produce phrases of music that combine jazz, new music, noise, and folk music into a new and organic whole would produce a musical composition made of complex relationships, causal chains, and combinatory effects that could only be traditionally notated by reverse engineering a score from the performance and could only be improvised by a group that was working with the same rigor as if they had a singular compositional vision. In other words, I'm proposing that we look toward creating music that represents the complex relationships of the everyday.

At the top of this essay, I specifically used the word manifesto. Manifesto presupposes a certain degree of wishful and utopian thinking, and the idea of a "mutual aid" complexity or social music is no different. While there are some using this approach already—Christian Wolff and Ryoko Akama's music and a recent *SA* contribution by Lester St. Louis (in *SA23*: The Alien Issue) come to mind—there are many questions still to be addressed. How do composers or performers communicate in a way that keeps the power balance equal? At what point does the freedom and community implied by an attempt at this kind of complexity become a term describing an autocratic or anarchic pursuit rather than a way of making humanly complex music? The idea is not perfect, and I've saved space that may have been spent on my concrete compositional approaches to the idea, but a manifesto is meant to be picked up by others, interpreted, and used to move things forward. I hope it will be and there will be an open exchange of ideas between composers and performers about how they have dealt with form, notation, decision making, and other performance practices in the future.

Finally, the question that should have begun this writing: Why? Why do I think it's important that we take seriously this specifically social way of generating complexity as one of the ways we structure music moving forward? When we engage in making music, we are practicing a form of society. This way of music represents the kind of culture I want. As great as our continuing musical traditions are, the act of faithfully reproducing a composer's score is monarchy at best, autocracy at worst, and when we freely improvise we are engaging in a kind of early pure democracy which only sometimes produce results that all involved are happy with. However, when we commit to a music that asks us to work together to make decisions that lift the group's efforts up above the composer or the individual performer's, we practice a kind of society in which the input of all is equally valued and the product is something that celebrates the best we have to offer.

A CONVERSATION
Audra Wolowiec with
Freya Powell

This interview took place in a small office booth at Parsons School of Design, where we both teach—a liminal space that seems appropriate to talk about the interstitial qualities of Freya Powell's work and her upcoming project, *Only Remains Remain*. We met having just become (working) mothers and over this past year have communicated in fragments and texts, checking in with each other about how to navigate the unknowns that surround our new roles. Freya's work engages with ideas of memory, loss, and how to record these states of being, oftentimes within the confines of political systems that include place, belonging, and otherness. She works fluidly across platforms from video, sound, installation, and performance, with undercurrents of writing and storytelling. The ways in which she uses the materiality of language to evoke voice, through slippages and gaps in translation, are especially inspiring as they are the elusive yet embodied qualities that I aim for in my own work with sound.

AW   I was listening to the recording of your rehearsal for *Only Remains Remain* on the train, as I traversed along the Hudson River, and was glad to listen without reading the script first. I knew a little bit about the project from speaking with you but something about being immersed in the "ocean of sound," as David Toop calls it,[1] seemed important for the first read. I heard both speaking and singing, words, phrases, and deconstructed syllables, and there was also a call and response that emerged, a layering of individual voices and a chorus. From reading the script afterwards, I became more aware of the language and various roles of each character. I wonder if you could talk about how you came up with the structure of the work?

FP   It's set up as a chorus of fifteen women, and if you think of a chorus in terms of classic Greek tragedies, they are a collective voice. So I think of each person, even though they are part of a collective, as having their own individual place that they're speaking from and they each are given an action word to keep in mind. When I wrote the script I was following the format of the chorus in *Antigone*, a parados, five stasimons, and then the exodus.[2] Each of the fifteen performers are each assigned a section that they are speaking from. The parados and the exodus (spoken by the first and fifteenth performers, respectively) are essentially the introduction and the conclusion, the backstory and the "where do we go from here." Then the lines of the five stasimons (the Ode to Man, the Ode to Hope, the Hymn to Eros, or Empathy, the Ode to Fate, and the Ode to Mourning) are divided amongst the remaining thirteen characters. That's how it was initially written, in this linear fashion, and then I cut it up. I interwove the lines but when each performer is speaking they are still speaking from the intention of their stasimon. I'm hoping that comes across when people experience it. It's probably more complicated than people need to know to get the gist. But that's the behind the scenes of it.

> AW You're translating the story, not retelling the story of *Antigone*, using translation as a framework to shed light on the current story of the U.S. border and the tragedy surrounding many of these border crossings. The lives that you're addressing are often unknown, putting into question the process of being honored and mourned after death, which is the crux of *Antigone*.

FP Instead of telling Antigone's story, I took the characters for how they behave in *Antigone* and then matched them to characters in the story on the border. In *Antigone*, Polyneices was the brother who, after he died, was refused any acts of mourning because he forged battle against the city. So, Polyneices becomes the migrants. Antigone, Polyneices's sister, believed that it was a crime to leave him unburied as his soul would wander forever and never find rest. She's the one who went to his side and began spreading earth across him, then returned to bury him. Within our story she represents the forensic anthropologists, the ones who are doing the exhumations and DNA testing to try to name the people and to hopefully, if possible, send their remains back home. For Ismene, Antigone's sister, I am taking her character from a French writer, Jean Anouilh, who reinterpreted *Antigone* and made it more contemporary. He framed Ismene as someone who understood what Antigone was doing but didn't want to join her because she was afraid of the repercussions. So, I am proposing Ismene as us.

> AW As the general public.

FP Right, we know that bad things are happening on the border but we aren't taking the steps to address it; even though we are implicated, we are not following through on it with any action. And then Antigone's uncle, Creon, is the state, the border patrol, the whole system.

> AW And the current presidency, too.

FP Yes, although this started back in the Clinton era.

> AW The lineage of that neglect.

FP Exactly. So, to return to your question about speaking and singing, the narrative is moving between the two. Most of the singing is actually a Greek translation from Anne Carson, the way she translated sounds of mourning when she translated *Elektra*, so it's "Oimoi, O Talaina, Pheu Pheu," which essentially translates to "Woe is me." I mean, there's no direct translation but that's, from what I know, as close as we can get.

AW   Does this have any relationship to Anne Carson's[3] interpretation of *Antigone*? I think, what is it titled, *Antigonick*? Where she writes, "How is a Greek chorus like a lawyer / they're both in the business of searching for a precedent / finding an analogy / locating an example / so as to be able to say / this terrible thing we're witnessing now is / not unique you know it happened before / or something much like it."

FP   This is from her translation of *Elektra*. The whole thing about this translation, the reason she uses the Greek even though she translated the work from Greek to English, is that it's the bodily utterances that are beyond language when you're in the state of grieving or mourning. That really resonated with me, and I was emulating that. We have four singers, two of which are opera singers. One is a mezzo-soprano and has this really grounding voice, she's the one who sings the "OiMoi." Each iteration is different as the singers are essentially improvising with each other. Though they each have their own adjectives, one will be a heavier one, and one would be a lighter, more haunting or eerie one.

AW   And I noticed, too, that in the singing, or parts of the singing that are overlaid with speaking, you hear it more as a sound, or as a layer. You don't always hear the complete words; it sounded as if there were phonemes or syllables or parts of words being voiced.

FP   Quite often when that happens, well, I love synonyms.

AW   Okay! (laughter)

FP   How else can I say this? I love synonyms. I love how words can be deeply related but also different, the meaning can bleed a little. So, often you'll see in the script that there will be a line and then a word listing happens of synonyms related to a word in one of the previous lines. When those happen, the outer chorus (the ones speaking) will be reading down the list and the inner chorus (the singers) are just extending that word from the same list. So that's why you're hearing syllables.

Freya Powell
Only Remains Remain,
Rehearsal, 2020

Freya Powell
Only Remains Remain
Script page 5, 2020

>   5.
>
> #2: Man, with all of his great accomplishments, is limited by his body.
> #3: While the body implies agency.
> #4: The body is bound by vulnerability.
>
> ENTIRE CHORUS -#2, 3, 4:
>   Susceptibility.
>   Mortality.
>   Inevitability.
>   *silence*
>
> #1: We recall Polyneices.
> ENTIRE CHORUS -#1:
>   Polyneices, decided to make the crossing.
>   Moved by desperation and guided by hope.
>
> #1: As Polyneices migrated north
>   he found cities that were previously passable...
> ENTIRE CHORUS -#1:
>   to be more patrolled,
>   more policed,
>   more surveyed,
> #1: more difficult.
>   *silence*
>
> ENTIRE CHORUS (TO THE AUDIENCE):
>   The Ode to hope
>
> #5: Hope, is a word of unknown origin.

AW   So it was just an elongated phrase or word that I was hearing fragments of.

FP   Yes, it was to add a little bit of color.

AW   Or like a tonal, visceral quality. That's also interesting in terms of synonyms and translating a text is that, while I don't translate texts, I would imagine if you were to try to find the word in English that encapsulates a word in another language...

FP   Especially in Greek or something like that!

AW   Right, something that doesn't even have a word in English, you search for the closest meaning. And it's not always about the direct meaning itself, but also how it *sounds*, and I think that's maybe why Anne Carson kept that phrase because it's more about the sound of it, and how it makes the body emote or feel when saying those sounds.

FP   Absolutely.

AW   There's this great article by Michael Cunningham where he talks about translation as a human act. He uses the first line in *Moby Dick* that begins "Call me Ishmael" as an example and breaks down the phonetics into their "musical" qualities: *Listen to the vowel sounds: ah, ee, soft i, aa. Four of them, each different, and each a soft, soothing note. Listen too to the way the line is bracketed by consonants. We open with the hard c, hit the l at the end of "call," and* then, in a lovely act of symmetry, hit the l at the end of "Ishmael."[4] What you're doing with this performance is similar in how you're conjuring and evoking mourning through not only what the language means but the way in which it sounds.

FP   Oh, how curious. I am not familiar with that text. I often come back to Lawrence Abu Hamdan's essay *The Aural Contract* in which he speaks about the bodily excess that accompanies the voice. He says: "This bodily excess of the voice resides not in its linguistic functions, but in its nonverbal effects; such as its pitch, accent, glottal stops, intonations, inflections, and impediments. As byproducts of the event of language, these effects reveal other kinds of evidence...." His research is much more clinical but I often think of this excess and hope to harness it to evoke mourning through the voice.

AW   When you are interacting with the actors and singers who are performing, in terms of being the director, what are some of the cues that you give or, how has that been for you to try to communicate these qualities of cadence and form? I imagine that you have something in your head, that you have already heard in a way, and that you're trying to give directives on how to bring that to life.

FP   It's difficult because it's the first time in this role for me, so I don't necessarily have the language—which we've talked a little bit about before. Even though I have an idea, it's more a sense or a feeling, than being able to be like "this is what I want." I'm not always able to necessarily point to what I want, and I feel somehow it's just that actors are amazing, just as a broad stroke, or I have been incredibly lucky with the people that I've been working with. I think that they have read the text and responded to it really well, they have a sense, and from interacting with me, they have given so much in terms of shaping the work, and probably responding to my facial expressions, you know?! (laughter) "Like, oh, that's happening, okay."

AW   And then dealing with it in real time.

FP   Right, it's a really exciting place to be in because I think for a lot of them, it's an unusual work, experience-wise it's varied. This is new territory for most of the performers. So somehow we have found this magical way of pointing to things and agreeing or not agreeing. I try to be as collaborative as possible, but sometimes I think "hmm, that's not right" and it's not going to work for me. They've been giving a lot to it, which has been great. I also have an amazing assistant on the project, Joy Salomon-Corlobe, who is an actor herself and a linguist. She has helped me navigate whatever distance I have in language with the actors. And, I have been lucky to have Samuel Lang Budin, an artist/musician, helping with the musical direction. It is truly an inspiring experience to be able to collaborate with them all—they somehow have read the work and intimately understand what I am after.

AW   Do you think it's different because it's experimental or because of the structure, or is it the content of the work itself? How do you think it's a departure from something that they might know or have done before?

FP   I think it's experimental, it's non-linear, it's interwoven, there is a lot of layering that happens.

AW   How has this process related to previous works, and especially with sound and voice? Your work is a lot about memory, and inviting people to participate in some way by telling a story, whether that's about a place or a site, or their own personal memory. So how has this been either a departure or continuation from these past works?

FP   It's definitely a departure in terms of working with actors and staging something that is happening in real time, versus mediated through a lens or through speakers.

AW   Or the process of editing.

FP   Exactly, or through a book, so this feels much more instant, in a way, or at least I imagine for an audience it will feel a lot more instant than having these things that have a form or a mechanism attached to them. So the similarities: I'm constantly interested in the question of "when is a life grievable?" and in sites that have been potentially overlooked or have these very strong histories that are just not necessarily known, or are not known very widely. I'm interested in how sites can hold memory. We tend to think of history as things, as data that is recorded, that is one voice. Whereas memory is more ephemeral, only existing on the lips of those telling. I am always working around the question of the individual versus the collective memory. When does an individual become a part of the collective memory? I think the way that the layering is happening in this piece first occurred in a more recent video project, which was a total departure from the way that I had been making videos. It's called "A Murmuring" and that was actually the first time that I engaged directly with a text. It has excerpts from *Hamlet* in it, and I worked with actors to do voice-over reading for that. That also has the same kind of synonyms, going back to synonyms! (laughter), a similar word listing, and through the editing process I did layer upon layer. It starts out with a conflict between what you hear and what you see, so the same list comes up as text on the screen, and then is in a different order from what you hear. So, it starts out slow and then there's this building up of visual and aural layers, which ends up building upon building upon building and feeling quite intense, where with other work, I tend to make things that are slower, and I want to say, *softer* almost—they evolve over time, whereas this felt much more immediate.

AW   Something that struck me both about your interpretation of *Antigone* and in some of your previous work is the physicality of the act of mourning, of being known and being put to rest, how this act is physical, and experienced by family members.

FP   As a closure.

AW   The idea that the soul will be at rest for the body or person themselves but also for the people who love that person, and it reminded me of that film *Nostalgia for the Light* [by Patricio Guzmán]. Have you seen that?

FP   You're the second person who has mentioned that to me.

AW   It's a heart-wrenching film that takes place in the Atacama Desert, where the women in the film are searching for the remains of their sons, from under Pinochet where their bodies were discarded, in a sense to bury the past without trace. But the Atacama Desert is also a place without clouds, because of the dry climate, so it's a site used to look at stars and outer space.

FP   It has a parallel narrative.

AW   Yes, you have people looking up at the sky through very large telescopes and then people looking into the earth and searching with their hands, for different things, for different meaning. There's something about the remains, finding a clue or a part of that person that is so important. These women can't stop, even though so much time has passed, they seem to be enveloped in the question that maybe, if we don't see the body itself, there's the chance that it didn't happen.

FP   I think that's the situation for a lot of people who have family members that are in that same situation, the forever not knowing if their loved ones have made it, that they could be somewhere, but you just don't know. From what I have read, it is just incapacitating.

AW   It's also this intangible thing, this form of searching—how do you try to get those qualities through with the performers or, how do you create that space of telling this kind of story? It's difficult, it's about other people in a lot of ways. Have there been some strategies of how to create that sense?

FP   There are a couple things. I keep telling the performers that we are all Ismene. No matter what we do, we are all Ismene. This is not our story. But we are implicated in it. We have a duty to some extent to be responsive, so I keep telling them that. In terms of finding that mental or emotional space, there's a circling that happens. In terms of movement and sort of "acting-ness," it is very minimal as I'm interested in the language, and the voices, and what the audience can perceive through bodily access. So there's not grand gestures happening or anything like that.

AW   It's to be listened to.

FP   Yes, and there are moments during the "OiMois," when the singers are holding the space of mourning, the performers will be circling and making gestures of mourning. The performance is immersive for the audience. There's an inner circle, and there's an audience, and there's an outer circle, and then more audience. There are moments when the outer chorus comes into that in between space and circles. In that moment they are all performing gestures that they've come up with, these manifestations of mourning. But minimal. I asked them to make small gestures of mourning, for themselves. Because the focus is not about the gesture, it's about what is happening with the voice.

AW   The subtlety and nuance almost reminds me of Pina Bausch,[5] a movement that isn't a huge display but is so emotional at the same time.

FP   Pina Bausch is a great example because she was someone so interested in the everyday actions, everyday gestures that we do, and this is very much a thing about how would you, what would be your daily mourning gesture, what would you be doing with your hands? With your body? Then a few of the singers are going to be shrouded and there will be moments when they unveil.

AW   Is that in terms of showing absence and presence, or?

FP   Absence and presence, and anonymity—they're not individual people, more in terms of coexisting.

AW   Or the collective unknown.

FP   Right.

AW   So in terms of the audience, will they have any role in intermingling or will the audience be seated around the performers?

FP   The only stage set is a mound of earth that the four singers will be around. Then about five or six feet out, there will be these gray benches creating a circle, and another five or six feet out, there'll be the outer chorus. The inner chorus will be in their spot in the center for the most part, and from the beginning when people are filing into the space, they will be holding a space through improvisation of an extended note. Then as the audience enters, they will be directed to either sit in the inner circle or they can stand around the outside edge. The outer chorus will be doing grid work. I don't know if you're familiar with this, I'm not even sure which acting school this comes from, but this notion of walking on a grid so that they are only able to go in straight lines and create 90-degree turns, not running into each other or running into the audience, and they'll be walking on the grid and performing these gestures of mourning, so they'll be moving through the space as people come in. Then once people are settled, they'll start walking in a circle around the interior audience.

AW   I love that because I think a part of what this really is about is empathy, and about understanding the struggle and the way that it's been neglected and the powerlessness, not just of the people involved, but of the average person to really do anything—and so implicating the audience seems important, even if they're not active participants, but just maybe to hear a voice coming from an odd angle or to be encircled by the performers.

FP   Right, they'll have to be actively moving around.

AW   There's something about when a performance is on a stage and you're sitting in front of the stage, there's a distance, one is removed from the action and can almost become a passive observer.

FP   A huge part of the structure is because we were working in the Dome at PS1, which is a circle, so then we were trying to figure out ways to address the sound of the dome, and having to struggle through how the way sound moves in the space, so we came up with the circle, and then we had to put the audience in the circle in order for the performers to be heard.

AW   Because of the reverberation of the space?

FP   Right, so we were working through this. I definitely like the structure for this because it's equalizing in a way, but we couldn't have that and then have the audience on the outside because then they're just watching this thing transpire and are not implicated. With them on the inside there are moments when the actors will be directly making eye contact and breaking the fourth wall, even though the fourth wall isn't in one physical plane, to directly address the audience.

AW   And this performance will happen in the gallery setting at PS1, and you'll keep the circular format.

FP   Yes, the sound will be so much better! The white noise was so much, like you're in an airplane hangar, or something.

AW   The recording you sent was pretty intense, just the way that the voice travels, I think it would be hard to control. I mean, there's something interesting about it, that you could probably play with, but it would completely alter the work.

FP   It would change it because, again, coming back to the language is what's important, the text is what's important, if it were about movement then there's infinite ways to play with that space in a beautiful way, but because I want the lines to be heard, by everyone, it got a little tricky.

AW   Something else that struck me about the project and your work in general were some of the influences that came up while listening. I know that writing plays a strong role in your work, stories that are both ancient yet parallel our contemporary experience, but also Janet Cardiff,[6] and I know you take your students on her *Sound Walk* in Central Park. The vocal installations of Susan Philipsz[7] too, I think it was her *Lowlands*, the recording installed in the tunnel, that sort of haunting quality came up when I was listening to the rehearsal. In certain parts the voices were dissonant, a little uncomfortable to listen to sometimes, and I think that's what she does with her own voice, not being a trained singer. There's something I really love about that because there's a tenderness to it, there's a vulnerability, you're being caught by surprise. There's something a little bit off about it, which I think has more power to communicate than something that's virtuosic. It's not about the skill of the singer, it's about the ability to communicate something human.

FP   I have no training in music, at all. I'm totally useless at that! (laughter) The singers will ask, what vocal range are you looking for? And I have no clue, I just don't know how to name it. But there's something, I'm always drawn to the voice. And I feel like, again, there's something unnamable, but deeply emotive. It can physically get you in a way, that I don't get by visual things alone, sometimes by movement I suppose, but it's just something intangible that gets you in the gut, and I would love to be able to harness that.

AW   There's also something that stays with a person and lingers. In terms of our visual culture at the moment, it's pretty fast and attention spans are so short, we see things and almost don't even spend time looking or hearing because we take in so much. But I think with the voice or sound, the haunting quality about it, is that it stays with you.

FP   It lingers.

AW   Yes, it has the effect or quality of memory, almost built into it in some way.

FP   I hope so!

---

1   David Toop, *Ocean of Sound: Ambient sound and radical listening in the age of communication*, Serpent's Tail, 1995.
2   (on what defines a parados or stasimons structurally...) The parados is essentially the entrance to the entire story. I am using it to set the foundation of the tragedy, the performer who is mostly speaking during this is leading us through the story, giving the background information. The exodus is the final scene or departure. The stasimons are historically when the chorus sings, also known as a "stationary song." Instead of creating a whole play with characters and a chorus, I have just taken the structure of the chorus to tell the story.—FP

3   Anne Carson is a Canadian poet, essayist, translator, and Professor of Ancient Greek. In addition to her many translations of classical writers such as Sappho and Euripides, she has published poems, essays, libretti, prose criticism, and verse novels that often cross genres. Her recent writing for *The Mile-Long Opera*, conceived by composer David Lang and architects Diller Scofidio + Renfro, co-written with Claudia Rankine, was inspired by real-life stories, gathered through first-hand interviews with residents throughout the city, asking what 7pm means to them. This was performed by 1,000 singers along the High Line elevated park in New York City in 2018.

4   Michael Cunningham, *Found in Translation*, The *New York Times*, Oct 2, 2010.

5   Pina Bausch was a German dancer and choreographer whose experimental movement-based work was often composed of repetitive, yet fluid, gestures that embodied everyday actions from intimacy to loss, with sparse stage sets ranging from domestic interiors and cafes to a floor covered in soil that stained the skin and clothing of the dancers. Her work influenced the field of modern dance from the 1970s onwards. "I'm not interested in how people move, but what moves them."—Pina Bausch

6   Janet Cardiff is a Canadian artist who works primarily with sound and installation, and is best known for her audio walks. "The format of the audio walks is similar to that of an audio guide. On the [binaural recording] you hear my voice giving directions, layered on a background of sounds: the sound of my footsteps, traffic, birds, and miscellaneous sound effects that have been pre-recorded on the same site as they are being heard. This is the important part of the recording. The virtual recorded soundscape has to mimic the real physical one in order to create a new world as a seamless combination of the two."—Janet Cardiff, from *The Walk Book*

7   Susan Philipsz is a Scottish artist based in Berlin who works with spaces, narrative, and sounds. "The song at London Bridge, *Surround Me*, can be interpreted as a cry from those who have disappeared beneath the waters of the river; and *Lowlands* is about the ghost of someone coming back to make a final farewell. 'I think people are fascinated by mortality,' concludes Philipsz. And, as we walk away, the sound comes after us, as if it doesn't want us to escape."—Lena Corner, *The Guardian*, 2010

2020 PART ONE: QUANTUM BLACK IN THE MOMENT

Composer: Moor Mother

Originally based on the parlor game *Consequences*, in which texts were assembled by guests without seeing (due to creative folding) what was previously written, *exquisite corpse* became an important source of collaboration and creative experimentation for surrealist writers and artists such as André Breton, Joan Miró, Tristan Tzara, and Marcel Duchamp. These artists used a form of the game as a way of assembling visual and textual ideas into a form that they could not have foreseen and, therefore, had very little control over. Some of the results were astounding, others less so. Every result, however, was something new.

Sound American's version of *exquisite corpse* adds a few twists in keeping with our milieu and mission. Each year, three composers will collaborate on a short work specifically for *SA*, to be published in that year's journals and recorded at the end of the year for streaming online. One artist will go first, passing on a set of information to the next who, in turn, will add, subtract, and change that information to create a new version of the piece before passing it on to the third, who will create a "final" take on the composition. The readers of *Sound American* will get to watch the whole process as it occurs as each version will be reproduced in subsequent issues.

We're very pleased to have the phenomenal artist Moor Mother as the inaugural composer of 2020's *exquisite corpse*. She gave us a powerful set of words that work as poem, rhythm, image, movement. From this, our next composer will work to shape their meaning in a completely new direction.

Many thanks to Moor Mother for providing us with *Quantum Black In The Moment* in the midst of a busy travel and touring period!

QUANTUM BLACK IN THE MOMENT

QUANTUM
THE BLACK
IN THE MOMENT
STACKED UP PARTICLES
REVERN LEON SULLIVAN
AERO SPACE AGENCY
NORTH PHILLY SATELLITE
DOX THRASH
PAINTS SHADOWS OF THE FUTURE
RIDGE AVE GATEWAY
FREE JAZZ HIGHWAY
LOW GROAN BUBBLING
COLTRANE STRAWBERRY MANION
A LOVE SUPREME
PLASMA THROUGH CONCRETE
THE PERSISTENT PAST
HIGH SCREECHING
FEEDBACK ROSETTA
LOOPING THE EVER PRESENT WAVE
QUANTUM
BLACK
IN THE MOMENT

FUTURISM

CAMAE AYEWA

Camae Ayewa, better known by her stage name Moor Mother, is an American poet, musician, and activist from Philadelphia, Pennsylvania. She is one half of the collective Black Quantum Futurism along with Rasheedah Phillips.

REG BLOOR

Reg Bloor is a veteran NYC experimental guitarist/composer known for her frantically dissonant solo work as well as her long tenure as Glenn Branca's Concertmaster/musician wrangler/right hand. She continues to run his ensemble and the label they founded together, SYSTEMS NEUTRALIZERS, where she recently released her second solo recording *Sensory Irritation Chamber* and Branca's posthumous *The Third Ascension*.

JOHN CORBETT

John Corbett is an American writer, musician, radio host, teacher, record producer, concert promoter, and gallery owner based in Chicago, Illinois. He is best known among musicians and music fans as a champion of free jazz and free improvisation.

JESSIE COX

Jessie Cox is a composer, drummer, educator and scholar, in pursuit of his Doctorate Degree at Columbia University. Currently residing in NYC, his roots are in Switzerland and Trinidad and Tobago. Jessie's work is centered around imagination-technology developments and rituals for reality re-rendering.

TAYLOR HO BYNUM

Taylor Ho Bynum has spent his career navigating the intersections between structure and improvisation—through musical composition, performance, and interdisciplinary collaboration, and through production, organizing, teaching, writing, and advocacy. Bynum's expressionistic playing on cornet and his expansive vision as composer have garnered him critical attention on over twenty recordings as a bandleader and dozens more as a sideman, notably through long associations with legendary figures like Anthony Braxton and Bill Dixon and forward thinking peers like Mary Halvorson and Tomas Fujiwara. He is currently the director of the jazz and creative music ensemble at Dartmouth College, where he also teaches composition and improvisation.

NAIMA LOWE

Naima Lowe is a visual artist and writer who comes from four generations of Black people who make things. She's steeped in a lineage of Black cultural production characterized by alchemic survival strategies known as collaboration and improvisation. Naima currently resides in Tulsa, OK where she is a Visual Art Fellow at the Tulsa Artist Fellowship.

PETER MARGASAK

Peter Margasak is a veteran music journalist who served as a staff writer for the *Chicago Reader* for more than two decades. He's currently writing a book about the cross-fertilization of Chicago's underground music scene in the '90s.

CHRIS PITSIOKOS

Chris Pitsiokos is a Brooklyn-based saxophonist, composer, and improviser. He has been praised by *Rolling Stone* for his "startlingly original vision" and "astonishingly fleet sax work." *Downbeat* has identified his band CP Unit as "A persuasive combination of harmolodic jazz and contemporary noise rock." As a soloist he has developed a unique voice on the alto saxophone, combining extremes in volume and amplitude, noise and lyricism, seamlessly.

LUKE STEWART

Luke Stewart is a NYC/DC-based musician and organizer. His bass playing has become an important presence on some of the most visible records of his generation, and his experiments have opened up a new context for upright bass and amplifier. He is also a radio producer, writer, cultural activist, and educator.

KEN VANDERMARK

Ken Vandermark is an improviser, composer, saxophonist/clarinetist, curator, and writer. In 1989 he moved to Chicago from Boston and has worked continuously from the early 1990s onward, both as a performer and organizer in North America and Europe, recording in a large array of contexts, with many internationally renowned musicians. In 1999 he was awarded a MacArthur Fellowship in music.

AUDRA WOLOWIEC

Audra Wolowiec is an interdisciplinary artist whose work oscillates between sculpture, installation, text, and performance with an emphasis on sound and the material qualities of language. She currently teaches at Parsons School of Design and Dia:Beacon. She is the founder and director of the publishing platform Gravel Projects.

NATE WOOLEY

Nate Wooley grew up in Clatskanie, Oregon and currently resides in Brooklyn, NY. He is a trumpet player, composer, and improviser. He also is the editor for *Sound American Publications* and the curator of the Database of Recorded American Music.

Imprint

FOR SOUND AMERICAN
Lisa Kahlden, President
Nate Wooley, Editor-in-Chief

2020 ADVISORY BOARD
David Grubbs
Rebekah Heller
Taylor Ho Bynum
Zeena Parkins
Matana Roberts
Ken Vandermark

2020 EDITORIAL BOARD
Lea Bertucci
Michael Dyer
Jennie Gottschalk
Marc Hannaford
Sarah Hennies
Charmaine Lee
Peter Margasak
Chris Pitsiokos
Lester St. Louis
Luke Stewart
Audra Wolowiec

ANTHOLOGY OF RECORDED MUSIC, INC., BOARD OF TRUSTEES
Amy Beal
Thomas Teige Carroll
Robert Clarida
Emanuel Gerard
Lisa Kahlden
Herman Krawitz
Fred Lerdahl
Larry Polansky
Paul M. Tai

DESIGN
Remake, New York

PRINTING & BINDING
die Keure, Brugge

Cover and p. 43 photos
by William Brower
Many thanks
to Thomas Stanley

SOUND AMERICAN PUBLICATIONS
20 Jay Street, Suite 1001
Brooklyn, NY 11230
Tel 646 442 7928
www.soundamerican.org

℗ & © 2020
Anthology of
Recorded Music, Inc.
All rights reserved.
No part of this book may
be reproduced or transmitted in any form or by
any means, electronic or
mechanical, including
photographing, recording,
or information storage
and retrieval, without prior
permission in writing
from the publisher.

ISBN
9781733333917